Praise for *The Growth Paradox*

"If there is an 'it' factor for books, this has it. *The Growth Paradox* is truly one of the most engaging, powerful books on entrepreneurship, life, and purpose that I have read, and I have read them all! It is personal, emotional, and practical and goes well beyond the 'how to' or war stories of most entrepreneurship books. This will be a must-read for all my students!"
—Al Danto, Senior Lecturer of Management, Entrepreneurship, Rice University Jones Graduate School of Business

"Reading *The Growth Paradox* was a truly transformative experience for me. As an entrepreneur facing the ups and downs of building my own business, it often feels like I'm on an island. But this book made me feel like I was not alone. The author's stories and insights were relatable and inspiring, and the practical advice provided a road map for navigating the challenges of entrepreneurship. If you're an entrepreneur or thinking about starting your own business, this book is a must-read."
—Nancy Almodovar, CEO, Nan and Company Properties, and Affiliate, Christie's International Real Estate

"Wow! If you are a beginner entrepreneur, this book hits you like a ton of bricks. Everything that was good enough to get here is not going to be good enough to get to the next step. This book is exactly what every business owner needs to hear to get over the three-million-dollar hump. Highly motivating and feels like someone is meeting you right where you are."
—Tarin Williger, President, Quality Cable Installers, LLC

"As a business owner for twenty years, I found *The Growth Paradox* insightful for the 'real' and not always 'intuitive' problems that I've experienced that were never taught in any school or college. It's not only a road map in building a successful business (and team), but it also exemplifies a 'keep it real' philosophy, which I believe most owners appreciate. I would recommend it to both new business owners as well as veterans who are struggling to achieve the type of success they deserve and want out of life."
—Troy Elmore, President, Impassioned Sales Solutions, LLC (authorized franchisee of Sandler Training)

"Teeming with insights, this remarkable book shows how you can infuse passion into all facets of your business. The leadership lessons offered here are shrewd—and the prose is convivial. As you turn these pages, you'll soon be reimagining what it means to support and motivate your employees—and you'll be captivated by the author's unflinching account of how she shepherded her company from its first to its second generation while navigating a complex father-daughter relationship. If you're looking to supercharge your passion-related battery and elevate your company's success, this book is for you!"
—Erik Dane, PhD, Associate Professor of Organizational Behavior, Washington University's Olin Business School

"*The Growth Paradox* will help entrepreneurs steer clear of the mind trash that is often allowed to happen in today's small businesses. The lessons in this book are simple, authentic, and required learning for growth-minded business owners."
　—Brandon Kinsey, Cofounder and Chief Talent Strategist, Kinsey Management

"If you own an SMB and want to break through that glass ceiling holding you back, the secrets are within you, as this astute guidebook points out. Straightforward and relatable, *The Growth Paradox* will resonate through practical examples of failure and success expressed in an enjoyable story. Highly recommended."
　—Scott Steiner, CEO, On-Target! Marketing

"It is clear that *The Growth Paradox* was written from the point of view of a business owner who has been in the trenches, made payroll, and gets that things can get messy. There are many books out there written by consultants who have never actually run a business, and the difference shows in the insight Jacky provides her readers."
　—Johanna C. Watson, President & CEO, Artemis Partners

"Insightful words from one who has built businesses from many phases. Real life advice for entrepreneurs and useful no matter what phase you are in. Jacky keeps the message real and digs into the real world of what it takes to grow a successful business."
　—Leah Afolabi, Owner, Urban Air Franchisee

THE GROWTH PARADOX

THE GROWTH PARADOX

Rethinking Control, Accountability, and Change to Move Your Business to the Next Level

JACKY FISCHER

Matt Holt Books
An Imprint of BenBella Books, Inc.
Dallas, TX

The Growth Paradox copyright © 2023 by Jacky Fischer

All rights reserved. No part of this book may be used or reproduced in any manner whatsoever without written permission of the publisher, except in the case of brief quotations embodied in critical articles or reviews.

Matt Holt is an imprint of BenBella Books, Inc.
10440 N. Central Expressway
Suite 800
Dallas, TX 75231
benbellabooks.com
Send feedback to feedback@benbellabooks.com

BenBella and *Matt Holt* are federally registered trademarks.

Printed in the United States of America
10 9 8 7 6 5 4 3 2 1

Library of Congress Control Number: 2023016851
ISBN 9781637744086 (hardcover)
ISBN 9781637744093 (electronic)

Editing by Katie Dickman
Copyediting by Michael Fedison
Proofreading by Denise Pangia and Ashley Casteel
Text design and composition by PerfecType, Nashville, TN
Interior graphics by Jeff Karon
Cover design by Siteseekers Graphics
Cover image © Shutterstock / petrmalinak
Printed by Lake Book Manufacturing

Special discounts for bulk sales are available. Please contact bulkorders@benbellabooks.com.

To my mom and dad. Even during hard times, they were a team. Not only did they dream of a better future, they dreamed of that future better together.

CONTENTS

Introduction — 1

PART 1: Is Your Kitchen Clean?

Chapter 1: What's the Point? — 9
Chapter 2: Prepare for Failure — 19
Chapter 3 Is Your Kitchen Clean? — 25
Chapter 4: Jack and Shirley — 34
Chapter 5: Zero Fucks — 41

PART 2: Building A Skyscraper? Start Digging!

Chapter 6: Begin with the End — 53
Chapter 7: Fail to Plan, Plan to Fail — 57
Chapter 8: Don't Be That Asshole — 70
Chapter 9: Don't Rely Solely on Financials — 82
Chapter 10: Running Fat and Skinny — 90

PART 3: Stop Holding People Accountable

Chapter 11: Nature of Accountability — 109
Chapter 12: Solo Accountable — 114

Chapter 13: When "Pretty Good" Is Bad   **118**
Chapter 14: Fire Top Performers   **122**
Chapter 15: Stop Helping   **133**
Chapter 16: Focus on Demotivating Employees   **142**
Chapter 17: Fragile—Handle with Care   **147**

PART 4: Do Less to Achieve More

Chapter 18: Trash Your Business Plan   **157**
Chapter 19: Build a Culture That Repels   **164**
Chapter 20: It's Not About You   **170**
Chapter 21: Ideas Kill   **186**

PART 5: Now What?

Chapter 22: Now What?   **197**
Chapter 23: Losing Money to Make Money   **203**
Chapter 24: To the Victor Goes the Spoils   **209**
Chapter 25: Change Is the Only Constant   **212**
Chapter 26: It's All Your Fault!   **218**
Chapter 27: Experience Not Necessary   **222**
Chapter 28: Two Tears in a Bucket   **228**
Chapter 29: The Daily Grind   **235**

Epilogue: John David Fischer   **237**
Acknowledgments   **241**

INTRODUCTION

THE LURE OF ENTREPRENEURSHIP

Many people, maybe most, have ideas for start-ups—and these brilliant ideas are based on passion and love: Home builders love to build; inventors love to invent. The popularity of TV shows such as *Shark Tank* demonstrate our fascination with the possibility that entrepreneurs might successfully sell their great ideas, moving those ideas out of their heads and into a successful business.

With a little luck and a lot of hard work, some of those businesses begin to make sales, and then it happens: The business becomes less about the brilliant idea and more about focusing on marketing, accounting, operations, human relations, and so on. Business owners spend less time on the passion that fueled their business and more time running their company. The founder might have started out with a passion for building homes but now spends over 95 percent of her time managing people, marketing her company, and keeping her books and records. Even the craftmanship of home building becomes less about creativity and more about consistency and quality control.

When the business moves away from the original passion, frustration can take over. At times, business owners liken a day at work to going into battle, fighting with customers and employees to get the job done. Then they come home from a long day's work exhausted and dejected, wondering how some business owners make it look easy. *What am I doing wrong? No matter how hard I work, I can't seem to take my business to the next level.*

When the romance of the new idea fades, business is business, which is why a company can bring in a hired gun who is a talented business leader to oversee a bakery or a manufacturing plant with equal efficacy. Savvy business leaders can move between industries successfully because they understand *business* rather than having particular artisan skills. Business fundamentals are the same in any industry, and these fundamentals are transferable if you have the discipline to learn and execute them.

Thinking about how to help others learn these fundamentals of growing a business led to my writing this book. *The Growth Paradox: Rethinking Control, Accountability, and Change to Move Your Business to the Next Level*, unlike the many others that crowd the business and entrepreneur genres, makes the skills required to build a multimillion-dollar company accessible to anyone with sufficient motivation to learn and implement its principles.

As you move from having a start-up mindset to developing into a mature business owner who is poised to scale, you will be shown the superpowers that will supercharge your business and create nonlinear growth. People often think that the extra "super" push they need to grow a company is to be more competitive and aggressive, yet most start-up business owners already have those skills. That is what got them in business in the first place. Instead, to grow your business, you will learn to spotlight the company's vision for the future rather than spotlighting yourself. You will learn how to empower your employees and align them with your goals. You will learn how to create an accountable, empowered team so that you can replace the day-to-day struggles that eat up your time with working on strategic goals to scale up your company.

BUSINESS SUCCESS IS MULTIDIMENSIONAL

There are over thirty million businesses in the US, and less than 1 percent will ever grow to over $10 million in annual revenue. Many companies that make the leap of over a million dollars in revenue stall out between $1 million and $3 million and around seven to ten employees. This is where people and processes begin to collapse if you don't have the right infrastructure in place. Artisan skills and passion aren't enough. While many business books tout having the magic key to success and focus on one or two components to unlock entrepreneurial success, issues are always multidimensional and require a leader's personal commitment in several areas.

The exciting part about running a successful, large company is that when you finally figure it out, it is like riding a bicycle: It becomes so easy that you almost forget about how much you struggled during the early years when the business was relatively small. Successful companies still have their ups and downs and wobble at times with new regulations, changes in the market, or leadership changes, yet a well-run company will hit these bumps along the way, stay upright, and keep on rolling down the road.

In 1985 my father, Jack Fischer, started 3 Men Movers, a residential moving company. I took over 3 Men Movers in the spring of 2003, ultimately buying the company from my dad in 2004. We currently have locations throughout Texas and are in the process of expanding nationwide. This book recounts the story of how 3 Men Movers started and the lessons I learned while growing up in the family business. The company has grown from one beat-up, sixteen-foot box truck and a few guys my father hired as helpers to one of the most successful and innovative independent moving companies in the nation.

Chances are you don't own a moving company. But 3 Men Movers was simply the conduit through which I gained my business knowledge—business is business. The principles I learned running a moving company can be transferred to your business. Someone once told me that, if it weren't for employees and customers, business would be easy—and this joke certainly rings true when an owner urges a group of people to row in the same direction when everyone has their own personalities and agenda, not to mention the challenge of keeping customers happy and returning.

This book will teach you what I have learned during my tenure of owning 3 Men Movers, including not only the techniques I used to grow the company to what it is today but also how the company grew me into who I am today.

A leader who seeks to transform a business must be open to being transformed by the business.

ACCOUNTING FOR SUCCESS

J. M. Barrie wrote, "I am not young enough to know everything," which sums up where I was when I returned to 3 Men Movers as a college dropout. In my twenties, I didn't know *anything* about business. I could not read a financial report, and I was clueless about leading people. I was a shy, artsy young woman who couldn't pass college algebra. I didn't have what people would call "leadership characteristics." I was an introvert, and still am, and lacked the discipline needed to run a company. Also, I learned my leadership skills from my dad, who was old-school and ruled with an iron fist.

I was confident, naive, and somewhat scattered due to my ADD. But what I lacked in experience, knowledge, and focus, I made up for with desire and drive. Looking back, I should have been more afraid when I took over the business, but my ignorance worked in my favor because I was fearless in my pursuit of growing the company. To put it bluntly, if someone with my lack of experience, education, and discipline can be an entrepreneurial success, so can you!

When I started working for my dad, there were only five people working in the office. 3 Men Movers has grown from $3 million in revenues to over $50 million. People have asked me how I do it, particularly small business owners who think that running a larger company must be much more difficult than running their smaller ones. But, counter to what most people think, operating a small company is a greater challenge because you don't have the human capital, structure, or processes that make things easy. Small business owners are usually so busy being the widget within their organization—trying to sell their product or services or trying to run the operations and keep the books and records—that they can barely keep their head above water, let alone work on their business's growth strategy. Often, they're strapped for cash and feel stretched in every direction. They feel stressed and stuck.

The Growth Paradox will help you get unstuck by preparing your business's infrastructure for rapid growth. To do so, I will show you how to increase the level of accountability throughout your organization, starting with *you*. Small business owners often focus on trying to maintain control of everything within their business so that the company doesn't make costly mistakes, but to move your business past the $3 million mark, you have to get comfortable with giving up control, making mistakes, and letting go of the need for things to be perfect. Think about Amazon founder Jeff Bezos. He isn't focused on the details and chained to a desk. He is literally able to leave the earth's atmosphere in a rocket ship and know that one of the world's largest and most complicated companies is being run well in in his absence. While you might not want to launch into outer space anytime soon, maybe you want to go on a family vacation and know that your company will be okay without you.

The concepts covered in the book are simple, but the execution takes discipline. Running a company is stressful at times, which is normal; however, most of the time, running a business should be challenging and fun. If you are stressed and feeling overworked, you are likely doing it wrong. When work is fun, and you are in the mental groove, chances are you are also growing and running operations more efficiently. Being successful always adds to the fun. Replacing the "I need to fight to get things done" mentality with "Through kindness and accountability, we can grow this company together" will have you ending each day still exhausted, perhaps, but also excited and ready for tomorrow's challenges.

ARE YOU STUCK IN A START-UP MINDSET?

I know your time is valuable, so take a minute and review the following questions. If you can answer "Yes" to any of them (as I once could), the following chapters will give you the skills to overcome the challenges you face as a small business owner so that you grow your business.

- ❑ People on my team are not accountable for their actions and often blame others for their mistakes.
- ❑ I am unable to take a few weeks off or spend time with my family without my employees blowing up my cell phone.
- ❑ I am consistently working over forty hours a week to keep up with everything. I could work weeks straight and still not finish my workload.
- ❑ People on my team leave for higher-paying jobs.
- ❑ As I grow, I have to hire new team members in a hurry, and often I feel like I'm over- or understaffed.
- ❑ I dread going to work in the morning. Work feels like a battle.
- ❑ We don't hit our goals regularly.
- ❑ My employees don't seem to care.
- ❑ My significant other feels second to the business and complains that I don't spend enough time on our relationship.
- ❑ I feel stressed, like I am running on a hamster wheel.
- ❑ I have limited time to adequately document procedures.
- ❑ Part of my daily job duty is to make sure everyone on my team is getting things done.
- ❑ I feel lonely. The weight of all my company's problems rests entirely on my shoulders.
- ❑ I can't seem to get to the next level.

DIRECTIONS FOR USE

The Growth Paradox is based on the lessons I learned from my experience scaling a small business. This book is broken into five sections.

- **Part 1: Is Your Kitchen Clean?** Scaling your business starts with you and your mindset. To get unstuck, you have to replace what you were doing with something new. But first, you've got to get your mind right to make the changes necessary to grow your business!
- **Part 2: Building a Skyscraper? Start Digging!** Start-ups are revenue focused. Owners are focused on generating more sales, so they often lose sight of creating a good foundation of processes. Even with revenue coming in, your growth plans won't succeed without a good foundation.
- **Part 3: Stop Holding People Accountable.** The biggest stress reliever for a business owner is having an accountable team. Accountable teams don't just happen; you have to nurture them in an environment that fosters accountability. This section will give you guidance on exactly how to create an accountable culture.
- **Part 4: Do Less to Achieve More.** A business owner's wild, risk-taking spirit that got the business up and running can be their biggest hindrance to scaling it to the next level. The adage tells us, "Hire accountable people and get out of their way!" But how do you turn that business cliché into reality?
- **Part 5: Now What?** Once your business has reached a mature phase, how do you deal with what comes next?

WATCH YOUR MOUTH

Business can be rough-and-tumble at times, and so is this book. I've made no attempt to be crude for pure shock effect, but sometimes a point seemed to call for a sledgehammer rather than a politely worded memo. Such colorful language often is passed between trusted friends—and I want you to feel as though we *are* friends.

So let's get fucking started.

PART 1

Is Your Kitchen Clean?

1

What's the Point?

DON'T DO IT FOR THE MONEY

As business owners, work is what we spend most of our waking hours consistently doing. Engaged business owners usually work long hours, and when we are not physically at work, we are still mentally engaged with our company. Whether we're in the shower, making our daily commute to the office, or lying in bed at night, we are actively working on ideas to improve our businesses. With all the time business owners devote to work, it is essential that we find satisfaction and meaning in what we do that reflects who we are as humans.

But what exactly does it mean to be human?

I clearly remember the ideas the Dalai Lama spoke about on a long-ago summer day. I was sixteen when he came to town to speak at Rice University. While I am not Buddhist, his ideas about what makes us human resonated with me. In particular, I was intrigued by his beliefs that humans are hardwired to be kind creatures. He explained that we don't have sharp incisors like wolves for tearing up flesh or claws like bears for killing. We were created to be gentle animals.

When you are running a business, at times you feel like you need fangs and claws to protect yourself (that is what you hire lawyers to do). A human's work environment should reflect his or her *kind nature*.

Speaking of which, a friend of mine, who had recently graduated from law school and taken a corporate counsel job, called me lamenting her day at work: "It is so stressful, but you know that is just how it is to be in business. The company is always in litigation because they are always doing shady things to make money. Business as usual, I guess."

This didn't strike me as "business as usual." Businesses don't have to be shady to make money. Not only *can* you create a win-win-win between the owners, employees, and customers, but, if you *don't*, your company will fail in the long term. A business is like a three-legged stool: You need all three legs to be strong to support the weight of a growing company. If someone is getting the losing end of the deal, employees will quit and customers will stop buying. And if business owners aren't making money, they will shut their doors and close down. Everyone has to win to create long-term success. To "win" means that all three—owners, employees, and customers—must receive value from the relationship. Business, at its essence, exists to create *value*.

You create value for your customer when you provide a service or a product that someone is willing to buy. You create value for your employees when you give them purpose in their work and pay them adequately for their contributions. Let's assume that you have a solid business model that, if well executed, will generate enough money after expenses to provide for you and your family to live comfortably. You may think that you have created value for everyone, including yourself.

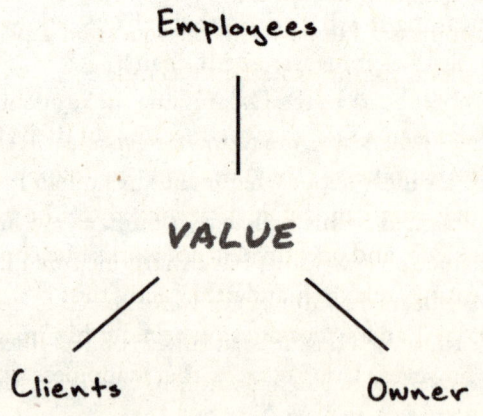

Business exists to create value.

But there must be more than just financial value for the owner. There needs to be emotional value too. Before you roll the dice and move past "Go," you must make sure your head is in the game. Your business should provide more than just money, which is only one part of the value relationship.

WORK IS PURPOSE

But work is work, *right*? Most of us are in the routine of going to work, going home, going to work, going home, enjoying our weekend, and then repeat. Maybe there is a vacation here or there; a holiday or a life event; or a birth, death, or wedding tossed in to mark the passage of time. Humans run on routines. Even if we have a nice routine, it can become monotonous. When it comes to work, we ask ourselves, "What is the meaning of this?" This question becomes ever more pressing if our routine is that of a stressed-out business owner.

In answering a question about the meaning of life posed by a waitress, the Dalai Lama said,

> "The meaning of life is happiness." He raised his finger, leaning forward, focusing on her as if she were the only person in the world. "Hard question is not, 'What is meaning of life?' That is easy question to answer! No, hard question is what make happiness. Money? Big house? Accomplishment? Friends? Or—" He paused. "Compassion and good heart? This is question all human beings must try to answer: What make true happiness?" He gave this last question a peculiar emphasis and then fell silent, gazing at her with a smile.[*]

While the Dalai Lama said that the meaning of life is happiness, his focus was on the path to happiness. How do we get to "happy"? If you look at the average person's day, you can divide it up roughly into thirds: One-third is work, one-third is sleep, and one-third is nonwork time consisting of caring for others, cleaning, eating, relaxing, and other activities.

I love the Dalai Lama's messages, especially his insights into the kindness of humans; however, I don't agree that happiness should be your goal.

---

[*] Douglas Preston, "The Dalai Lama's Ski Day," *Reader's Digest Canada*, June 14, 2016, https://www.readersdigest.ca/culture/dalai-lamas-ski-day/.

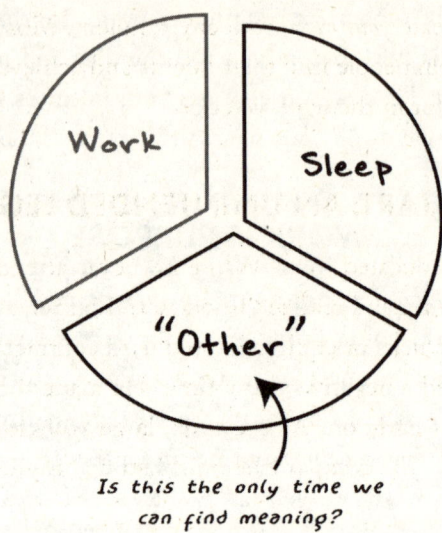

Happiness as a goal is hard to achieve because it is fleeting in nature. Instead of seeking happiness in your work, consider aiming for *purpose*.

YOUR SPECIAL PURPOSE

Viktor Frankl, the author of *Man's Search for Meaning*, believed that people find meaning in life through finding a purpose for their existence. He theorized that one of the ways we find meaning in our lives is through work, which can give us a deep feeling of purpose. However, jobs that we hate can suck out the very marrow of life, propelling us into a deep depression.

We may think that the route to happiness is through the pursuit of success, including business success, but as Frankl pointed out, "Success, like happiness, cannot be pursued; it must ensue, and it only does so as the unintended side effect of one's dedication to a cause greater than oneself or as the by-product of one's surrender to a person other than oneself."

Being a business owner is rewarding because you are in a unique position to have a positive impact on so many people's lives. Not everything I do at work is purposeful, and not everything I do at work brings me happiness, but I find that being in a position of leadership brings a deep sense of meaning to my life. When you are a business owner, you have the opportunity to create your own culture based on your unique values. You get to hire the people *you* want to work with and create *your own* work environment. Most of all, as a business owner, you get to help people find their talents and achieve great things. What more could you ask for in the work you do?

MY START: AN UNINTENDED LEGACY

My dad was a self-educated man. While he never attended college, looking back at his business model, I realized he was a trailblazer, ahead of his time. He didn't own moving trucks or equipment and used contractors to do the moves, which was considered a negative at the time. He made the decision to sell the trucks to the movers early on. At the time, large trucking companies owned huge fleets of trucks. The company he built had no tangible assets and its sole value was its brand.

Thirty years later there is Uber, the largest taxi service that owns no cars; Airbnb, the largest vacation rental that owns no rooms; Facebook, the largest online content manager that creates no content; and many other large, assetless companies, but back then companies held fixed assets. The negative aspect of the model, at the time, was that most of the value of a business was based on fixed assets. While my dad's business was successful, meaning it cash-flowed, it didn't have any assets of value on the balance sheet.

In 2002, my dad suffered a massive stroke, and his slow recovery hampered his ability to take the company to the next level. His manager took advantage of the situation and wasn't putting much effort into her work. His CPA also tried to take advantage of the situation and offered to purchase the company for $750,000, which was undervalued. My dad was at a crossroads. He reached out to me, asking for me to come in for a few weeks to help evaluate his company and advise him on what to do next. At the time, I was a young mother and attending college as an arts major. I knew little about business, yet saying no to my dad was not an option, and so I started working for him the next week.

At first, I just hung around, taking notes and asking questions. I went through all the data I could find. I tried to get a feel for the company. After a few weeks, it became difficult to just be a bystander: I noticed little things that needed to be done, and instead of evaluating the company, which was what I was hired to do, I rolled up my sleeves and got to work.

I started with simple tasks, such as making sure that we answered the phones within the first few rings and that the team showed up on time and worked their scheduled shifts. I refereed disputes in the office and cleaned up clutter. The revenue began to increase slightly, and the business started to run more smoothly; soon, weeks turned into months and I was still there.

When we started making more money, I was excited. The changes I made weren't based on my amazing business skills as much as common sense. Anyone who cared about the company could have figured these things out. I still didn't know how to read an income statement. I had no idea of the concept of amortization or depreciation. I had a *lot* to learn, and this was before the Internet. I spent afternoons at the library checking out books on business accounting.

Though I wasn't an effective leader in the first few years, at least I cared, which the previous manager hadn't. My work ethic rubbed off on other people in the office, and everyone picked up the pace a bit. While we didn't have a clear direction, we were working with increased conviction. I started out trying to be a tough leader, like my dad, but soon my natural leadership style, a style different from my dad's, began trickling through. I was less of an autocratic leader and more of a nurturer, and the movers were receptive to this kindness and responded with more dedication and hard work.

As time passed, I decided that although I liked my job, I did not like working for my dad since our leadership styles clashed, often resulting in me getting yelled at in front of the other employees. We just couldn't get along. I decided that, for the sake of my relationship with my parents and my own sanity, the best solution would be for me to quit my job working at 3 Men Movers. But the thought of broaching the subject with my father scared the hell out of me since I had never said no to him before.

I scheduled a meeting with my dad and before the meeting I practiced what I was going to say to him for hours in front of the mirror. "Dad, I appreciate the opportunity you have given me but I think our relationship as father and daughter should come before work—" My careful practice for delivering the news quickly went to pieces when he cut me off mid-sentence: "The hell with you!" he shouted. "I don't need you anyway." He waved his hand at me to leave and pointed toward the door.

I left the office that day crushed. I thought his response was just mean. Looking back at this moment as an older and wiser adult, I realize that my leaving was a rejection, which hurt him. My dad dealt with pain by getting angry.

After I left, his previously calm life began to fill up with the day-to-day issues of running a small business. My mom, who wanted me to come back to the family business, went on strike and refused to cook for him until he called me. The final straw broke when at the weekly meeting the drivers signed the back of a yellow invoice and gave it to my dad as a petition to get me to return.

My dad relented and called me to ask if I would come back to run the company. I told him that I would return under the condition that I could buy the company. He reluctantly agreed, setting the price at $2.7 million. I naively thought I could take the business financials to the bank and they would write me a check for $2.7 million to buy the company.

I put on a suit and high heels and visited nine banks. I filled out applications and met with bankers. Each time, an enthusiastic loan officer seemed excited about loaning me the money, but when they took the loan application to the underwriters, I was rejected.

From my perspective, I thought it was a great deal for the bankers. I had run the business for a year, and I was doing a decent job. The company had an eighteen-year track record of success. It cash-flowed and had an established brand name. What wasn't there to like?

From their perspective, the only reason I was in the position to buy the company was that my dad was the owner. I had no business experience, and our drivers were owner-operators, so the company didn't own any trucks to leverage as collateral. I couldn't answer even simple business questions intelligently. As far as they were concerned, I was all hat and no cattle.

I thought they were being unfair and didn't understand my value. I even wondered if maybe the bankers were sexist. I look back now and realize that the bankers would have been damn fools to loan me so much money.

I went back to my dad with my tail between my legs and had to tell him that I could not raise the money to buy the company. He said, "I never liked bankers anyway!" With that, he financed the entire amount at a 6 percent interest rate, which was to be paid back monthly over the next fifteen years.

On October 29, 2004, the lawyers wrote up the documents, and I signed the note and became the owner of a business.

Making the loan payment to my parents was the most important check I wrote each month for fifteen years. It was due on the first of the month, not the second or the third. If we had someone new in Accounting and it was even a day late, I would get a phone call from my parents wondering what happened. My parents don't play around.

The challenge of paying my parents that huge monthly bill was a big driver of my success. I was directly responsible for my parents' retirement. My parents had worked hard their whole lives and were finally successful in creating a profitable company. They were putting all their trust in me, and failure was not an option: That was my "Why." My pain was the fear of potential failure, which pushed me far out of my comfort zone. I was motivated by the fear potentially ruining my family business, my parents' retirement, and my dad's legacy. I couldn't screw this up!

A NEW BEGINNING

The petition the drivers signed meant something to my dad, convincing him not only to ask me to come back, but also giving him the confidence to sell his company to me. Later he and my mom added their signatures, under the movers' names, and had it framed for me. Today, it hangs proudly in my office as a reminder of my obligation to my workers, for if it weren't for them, I would have never had this opportunity.

But why did the drivers sign a petition to bring me back? My dad had been running the company successfully for eighteen years. I am sure a change to a younger, less experienced leader had to be a decision they didn't take lightly. I realize now that the movers' signatures on this petition wasn't just a reflection of what the movers liked about my leadership, but was also a rejection of an old-school, autocratic style. The signatures signaled their desire to shift to a new style of leadership based on humility and kindness. They saw something in me that I wasn't even aware of myself.

REFLECTING ON YOUR TRUE PASSION

One night, when I was at dinner with a friend and fellow business owner and his teenage children, he gave them the fatherly lecture about finding a job that fulfills their passions. His son quipped back, "Dad, are you passionate about manufacturing electronics?" His son's comment caught him off guard, but he recovered and said, "I am passionate about owning my own business. I am passionate about people."

I never dreamed of owning a moving company, let alone *enjoying* it. When I was a child, the last thing I wanted to do was run a household moving company. I fancied myself a starlet and spent hours getting dressed up and producing musicals in the living room for my parents, once creating an entire musical around the Styx *Paradise Theatre* album. As a teenager, I would stand in front of the bathroom mirror putting makeup on, and my dad would walk by and yell, "Focus on what you are putting in your head, and not on your face! Put that shit down and grab a book!"

Now, I run a moving company, and I love what I do, even though no one can say that moving furniture is a sexy business. I enjoy being part of the moving industry because I like the idea of helping people, and who needs more help than people in the middle of their move?

I also get to hang out with people I care about and respect. I am selective about the people on my team. I'm protective of the culture we are continuously creating. Filling my company with happy, engaged people and creating processes that eliminate unexpected and unwanted surprises fills me with purpose. I shy away from drama and chaos, and I value peace in my life. Call me a *hippie capitalist*! I love helping people, and I love the challenge of making money—I know that the two don't have to be mutually exclusive.

At the time my dad had a massive stroke, there were only a few people working in the office. Due to his health, he had become an absentee owner, and the culture he had built was beginning to crumble. His business model was solid and profitable, but the company lacked the infrastructure it needed to scale. I worked long, stressful hours in the beginning of my tenure. My days felt like the arcade game of Whac-A-Mole: For every problem I clubbed down, three more instantly popped up.

Because I was in love with the idea of exciting change, I constantly bombarded my team with my newest idea, and, as a result, we started many projects that we never finished. I found regular meetings boring, so I constantly scheduled and rescheduled them. Everyone ran around in different directions, and the company lost money and opportunities due to my poor management and execution.

Out of necessity, I quickly grew into an effective leader who focused on the company's vision, who learned how to empower employees, who avoided

Whac-A-Mole crises, who ran the company efficiently, and who had more time to enjoy being a business owner instead of feeling stressed and worn out.

Ask yourself the following: *Does your work give your life meaning?* This philosophical question has to be addressed before any of the others can matter. If the answer is no, what would give your life meaning? I am not saying running a business can be as good as bacon, chocolate, and sex every day, but don't look back years from now and wish that you had done something else in your life.

I've heard people say that *regret* is the saddest word in the English language, and I agree.

If you don't have passion for what you do, chances are you won't be successful. If you heard that the restaurant business was a good business to get into, yet you have no passion for food and serving people, how will you compete with someone who does? A competitor who loves what they do and brings that love with them to work every day will be a hard person to beat. Passion is infectious, and your employees and customers can tell if it is lacking. You've got to have your mind right if you want to scale your business.

END OF CHAPTER CHECKLIST

Use this list to get your mind right:

- ❏ Am I the company's biggest cheerleader? (I hope you answered, "Yes!")
- ❏ I am still running the company in ten years. How does that make me feel? (If the feeling is dread, you should examine if running this business is something you want to do long term.)
- ❏ Is there something I would rather do, something I have a passion for, besides running my existing company? (Imagine your perfect workday, and make sure it aligns with your actual workday. Are you stuck behind a computer when you want to be social? If you are creative, does your work fulfill your need to be creative?)
- ❏ Am I just doing it for the money? (If your answer is "Yes," go on a vacation to get away from daily work and instead work on mapping out a future life that brings you joy.)

2

Prepare for Failure

There is an old story about a man who went for a walk every day. When he passed his neighbor's house, he would hear a dog howling loudly from the front porch. After a few days of hearing the dog howling, the man walked up to his neighbor and asked, "Why does your dog make so much noise?" The neighbor replied, "Because the dog is sitting on a nail." The man was confused and asked, "Why doesn't the dog just move?" And the neighbor responded, "Because it doesn't hurt enough."

During my first year as a CEO, I found an executive mentoring group called Vistage, and I stayed in that group for fifteen years. My group consisted of eighteen business owners who met monthly and discussed problems that occurred in our business. We called it "Processing Issues." During this time, we were able to get feedback from our peers on issues we were trying to solve, helping us navigate the troubled waters of running a small company. I discovered three surprising things during these meetings:

1. The overwhelming majority of the owners were not at all in the dark about the issues in their businesses. They knew exactly what was wrong and what was preventing their company from scaling.

2. What was even more interesting was that not only did they know exactly what their issues were, they usually knew exactly what they needed to do in order to fix the problem.
3. Even though they knew what was wrong and how to fix it, most were not pursuing any positive actions that would begin solving the problem.

Why weren't they doing anything to address the problems in their company? I am qualified to answer this question because I was one of the people in the group who brought up issues that, deep in my gut, I already knew how to solve. And here is the answer: *because the pain wasn't great enough to create action.* We were like the dog sitting on the nail.

Ask yourself right now the following questions:

1. Am I reluctant to fire someone on my team who clearly is holding us back?
2. Do we have a process that is broken and is creating issues?
3. Have I delayed hiring for a position that would help make the company run more smoothly?

If you answered yes to one of the questions above, your pain isn't significant enough to create change. To scale your company, you need to make changes. If not, the old motto applies: *If you do what you always do, you will get what you always get.* The changes you need to make to grow your company are scary, and generally won't happen unless you feel enough pain to push you to do something different.

I am deathly afraid of heights. If someone asked me to bungee jump, I would say, "Hell no!" If someone offered me a suitcase full of money to make the jump and asked me again, I would still say, "Hell no!" If someone said they were going to throw my children off the cliff if I didn't jump, I would leap off the cliff in a swan dive before they finished the sentence. My example is dramatic, but you get the point.

To make changes, the stakes have to be high enough to push you out of your comfort zone. Unfortunately, the push you need might stem from a life-changing event: a spouse who says they can no longer be second to your company and files for divorce; cash-flow issues that threaten to close your company down; the loss of some critical employees; or your retirement looming in the near future and your concerns about not being financially ready.

Perhaps you are questioning your purpose in life and wondering whether being a business owner is for you—you have decided to "scale" your company and sell. Maybe you are at your wit's end and are tired of being overworked and stressed all the time. The exact reason that gets you to the point of change is less important than the fact that you take action to change when you need to. If you are not ready, you will settle for business as usual.

FROM PAIN TO CHANGE

You need to be willing to move forward and act on your current issues. No book by itself can do this for you, but if you are willing to push yourself out of your comfort zone, the ideas in this book will help you move forward. The changes necessary for a long-term strategy can be painful at first, but they are part of the process.

Things That May Get Worse Before They Get Better

1. Increased overhead expenses
2. Increased work hours for you and others
3. Upset teammates (often with you as the recipient of their anger)
4. Teammates who quit or need to be terminated
5. Confusion
6. Negativity
7. Decreased profits
8. (Add more horrible stuff here that I haven't even thought about.)

These side effects of change are scary, but part of business is making short-term sacrifices for long-term gain, as most of us have had to do in other areas of our lives. Perhaps, in order to buy your first car, you had to skip dinners and movies for what seemed like forever to save up the money for the down payment. Or, when you decided to lose weight, you had to fit your 5 AM workout into your morning schedule and stop eating your favorite foods. Or, even for the simple act of cleaning out the garage, you sacrificed your weekend and pulled everything out onto the driveway. Remember all the things lying in the driveway? Like cleaning your garage, when you pull everything out to sort through, things will get a whole lot messier before they get better.

You wouldn't be where you are if it weren't for the sacrifices you made along the way. Creating change within your company is no different. You and your team will be challenged and pushed out of your comfort zone. Growth can be messy.

COMFORT IS THE ENEMY

Many business owners have a "lifestyle" business that makes enough money to support their comfortable lifestyles, which is fine if that is your goal. However, when business owners are too comfortable, they often become resistant to change.

> *The biggest enemy of change is comfort that breeds complacency.*

If you are a new business owner, you are more likely to be open to change. After all, you haven't developed years of habits that have prevented you from scaling. However, if you have owned your business for years and are still answering "Yes" to some of the questions at the end of the previous chapter, then you have to ask yourself, *What it is going to take for me to make a change?*

DON'T STEP BACK FROM THE EDGE

You are on the edge of making big changes, but you don't think you can jump. You look over the edge, and everything seems too scary. It is safer to keep things the way they are, you think. You start overthinking and playing the "What If" game. Business owners are usually smart and analytical, and those traits can come with the extra baggage of analysis paralysis, the fear created by overanalyzing what could happen, which prevents you from moving forward. The more you know, the more fearful you become.

If you only listen to your cautious brain, you might never have started a business in the first place—after all, if you consider all the possible things that can go wrong and the failure rate of new businesses, you would be crazy to start a business. But you did! Now, it is time to make changes in that business to grow it to the next level.

> **Ask yourself how far you would be willing to take your business if you knew you would not fail.**

My dad didn't allow his fear of failure to prevent him from taking risks. His propensity to act quickly, sometimes too fast, is probably why many of his early businesses failed, but ultimately it is also why he finally achieved success: With every failure, he got back up. He never quit.

When he was able to keep one moving truck busy with work, he went to the bank to ask for a loan to purchase four more. The bank rejected my dad's loan request. So, over the next few years, we stopped spending money on anything except necessities, reinvesting every penny saved back into the business.

When we finally could have afforded to upgrade our lifestyle and buy a new car and move into a nicer apartment, we didn't. My parents continued to share a beat-up 1980 Plymouth Colt hatchback, and we didn't move from the small apartment we rented in a rough neighborhood. My dad even decided to stop using the air conditioner in the summer and the heater in the winter to save money. For those of you who don't know Houston's weather, it gets to be well over one hundred degrees in the summer, but my father figured that since people did not have air-conditioning when he was young, air-conditioning was a "luxury." And we would heat the apartment during the freezing winter by turning on the hot water in the shower and pointing the nozzle toward the tile wall while leaving the shower curtain open so that steam would come rolling out of the bathroom and steam-heat the house. The apartment manager constantly wondered why the wallpaper in our bathroom started curling up and sliding off the walls and had to be replaced so often. Dad had a vision to grow his company, and saving money to buy these trucks was part of the plan.

We continued to save our money to reinvest in my dad's dream. As a family we made short-term sacrifices to invest in his long-term dream. We figured out how to live off of my mother's steady but minimum-wage paychecks and used my dad's income to grow the business. We learned how to make meatloaf last multiple meals by adding a lot of oatmeal to the recipe. We learned which grocery stores would triple your coupons.

My parents were in their fifties and still were living paycheck to paycheck and barely scraping by. We were usually one step ahead of having our utilities shut off, and then sometimes we weren't, and I would come home from school to a dark apartment.

My dad was smart, but that didn't get in the way of him taking risks. Most of his life, he was a paycheck away from being homeless, and there is nothing like a good dose of poverty to kick you in the ass and get you moving.

END OF CHAPTER CHECKLIST

Are You Ready to Scale?

If any of the following statements ring true, you might be complacent and unwilling to embrace the discomfort it takes to make the changes needed to grow your business. Remember, success breeds complacency.

- ❏ My business has become a lifestyle business, and I'm too comfortable to take the risks to grow.
- ❏ I can pinpoint problems with people on my team as well as with broken processes, yet I'm not willing to take the steps needed to fix them.
- ❏ I need to hire someone who can take my business to the next level, but I don't want to make the sacrifice or personally take a "pay cut" to fund that hire.
- ❏ I am not willing to make short-term sacrifices to create long-term gain.

3

Is Your Kitchen Clean?

I was born in Dixon, Illinois, a small farming community. As a child, I was a bit lazy, though not unusually so for my age. This drove my dad mad. The issue stemmed from my dad's lack of parenting skills; children's age-appropriate behavior was something my dad never quite understood. He expected a child to pop out of the womb with perfect manners, consideration for others, a ferocious work ethic, and a sense of accountability. Just ask anyone with a two-year-old—children are not born that way. You have to teach them how to share and how to be nice. You also have to teach them about accountability.

In business, as in life, you must honor your commitments. Accountability starts with the business owner, and entrepreneurs have a reputation for often being flighty. If you want your employees to be accountable, it starts with accountable leadership. Many people struggle with accountability because they choose instant gratification over honoring their commitments.

SNOOZE-BUTTON NATION

Now, with advances in technology, it seems like our nation has put significant value on convenience and instant gratification over getting the job done. We want everything now, and we don't want to work for it, or at least not that hard. We want immediate fixes, an easy button, a pill, a shortcut. We have become a nation of fast food; fad diets; get-rich-quick schemes; pills that promise us happiness, better sex, no pain, and more sleep; and we can become "friends" with a click of a button on social media. While some advances are good, sometimes there is no substitute for doing things the old-fashioned way.

What does that mean for accountability? Accountability takes sacrifice and effort. It means that we can't have our instant gratification of enjoying a TV show when we need to shut it off and get to work. It means we have to sacrifice the things *we want to do* for the things *we said we were going to do*.

Let's start with one of the most basic things we all do daily: getting up in the morning. Do you set the alarm before you need to wake up, knowing that you will hit the snooze button? Many people set their alarms for 5:30 AM when they need to wake up at 6 AM. They will hit the snooze button to feel the instant gratification of a few extra minutes of sleep. They will continue to hit snooze until about six fifteen, when they finally get up. By then, they are running late and feeling frazzled. Wouldn't it be easier to set the alarm for 6 AM and get a deep, uninterrupted sleep until that time, then possess the discipline to wake up immediately without procrastination? Instead, in the first moment of a new day, we start in procrastination mode. We have become an undisciplined, snooze-button nation.

COMPLETING WHAT YOU STARTED

My dad was big on kids doing chores. After my older siblings moved out when I was five, the chores fell on me. It was my job to wash the dishes. Even though we had a dishwasher, I was forbidden to use it. My parents used the dishwasher to store potatoes and onions, perhaps saving on electricity in the process.

One night when I was seven, I had hand-washed the dishes, dried them, and put them away, but I had forgotten to wipe down the counters. After dinner, my dad went into the kitchen to grab a beer from the fridge and found a lump of butter with breadcrumbs stuck in it on the counter, which was entirely unacceptable to him. When we moved from Dixon to Houston, we moved into a squalid apartment complex, and one clump of butter left out overnight would create a rush of roaches from all the roach-infested apartments adjacent to ours, ready for a feast.

When he noticed the butter, he shouted for me to come into the kitchen. He pointed to the yellow lump and bellowed, "What is this?" I stared at him with big eyes, too afraid to answer, but he once again yelled out his philosophy of accountability: "Do what you say you are going to do! You were supposed to clean the kitchen. Does this kitchen look clean?"

In times of frustration like these, he would make a growling noise and rub his eyes by grinding his fists into his face with his middle finger sticking straight out—the finger was dislocated in a machine while he was working on an assembly line back in the 1950s. His boss at the time wanted him to cut the dislocated finger off because he feared it would slow down my dad's productivity on the assembly line. My dad refused, so his middle finger permanently stuck up as a kind of "Fuck You" to "The Man."

My relationship with my dad was one of extreme contrasts. He was both the most influential person in my life and also my main antagonist for the first thirty years of my life. He was feared, admired, and loved, and also the person who taught me the most about ethics, respect, and how to persevere. He was a functioning alcoholic while at the same time possessing a strict German work ethic. He woke up on time and never missed a day's work.

When he yelled at me in the kitchen, I was frozen, unable to muster any response, not even a "No." But I started to make a connection in my head about what counted as a complete, finished job. Throughout my childhood, my dad repeated endlessly, "Do what you say you are going to do, or don't say it." And the advice sank in.

In business, accountability starts at the top. Unfortunately, entrepreneurs have a reputation of starting multiple projects and not completing them. Take inventory of how you handle projects. You will lose credibility with your team if you don't finish what you start.

ARE YOU ACCOUNTABLE?

Former Starbucks chairman and CEO Howard Schultz eloquently said something similar to my dad's advice: "Under-promise and over-deliver." However you choose to phrase it, accountability starts with you because *you* set the standards, both good and bad, for everyone to follow.

To run a quality organization, you must have accountable people on your team, and as a leader, you must start by looking in the mirror to access your own accountability.

Accountability is a trickle-down value. Show me low-accountability business owners, and you can bet on it that their direct reports are low in accountability too. Lack of accountability at the top trickles down to frontline workers not being accountable to customers. And what do high performers do when their boss suffers from low accountability? High performers get fed up and leave! The result is a company left with low-accountability people. While you might value accountability, your actions are what your team will see.

Are you mirroring the type of behavior you want your team to follow?

The business owner's actions sets the values of their entire organization.

ADDICTED TO CHAOS

A business owner from my business group told us that the people in his organization understand who he is, and they accept him that way. They know he overcommits himself. He shows up late for company meetings, cancels 1-2-1 mentorship meetings, and, like unpredictable weather, will change the entire company's direction at any given minute, causing a wake of chaos in his path. He shrugs off his low-accountability behavior as merely being *who he is*, and something that his team members are "OK with" because it is a part of his being fully self-expressed.

If you think about it, what choice do his people have? They can either accept the business owner—their boss—or find another job. That doesn't sound like much of a choice.

I recognize this type of owner because I used to be just like him. I didn't have regularly scheduled meetings. I also canceled 1-2-1s with my staff for "more important" things. But what could be more important than mentoring someone on my team? At the time, I hadn't matured enough to understand that the correct answer was "*nothing*." I ran the company based on the exciting idea

I came up with on that particular morning. It felt good for me to be me—I can run that way. I liked pivoting ninety degrees and creating chaos. The chaos from change felt exciting.

Unfortunately, I found that this wasn't the case for my team. I thought I was energetic and dynamic. They thought I was a flake and scattered. I thought the pace was fast and thrilling. They thought the pace was grueling and draining.

I always had good excuses for my behavior. I told myself these were normal characteristics of an entrepreneur—starting projects and not finishing them and flying by the seat of my pants. I should embrace these eccentricities, right? I am who I am.

While it is true that entrepreneurs are often inherently risk-takers, and being a risk-taker can be crucial when starting a business, this isn't the type of behavior that will help you grow your business.

AN ACCOUNTABILITY EQUATION

How do you become more accountable in your business? Follow the Accountability Equation:

$$Say = Do^*$$
$$^*always$$

What you say every day at the office should match your actions (*always*).

If Say ≠ Do*, then there are only two ways you can fix the equation. You have to change one or both sides of the equation so that they become equal.

1. Increase the "Do." Start doing everything you say you are going to do.

   Or

2. Decrease the "Say." Stop saying you're going to do so much.

Let's walk through an example of when you should say less. You have committed to working on a project for your teammate, but you have social engagements that evening. Do you abandon the project? You already worked ten hours, so perhaps you stop working on the project in favor of the party and miss the deadline.

It isn't that you're lazy—you've been working sixty-hour weeks. You're exhausted and need and deserve the social break. But when the teammate asked for your help, it felt so good to say, "I can get that to you tomorrow." Instant gratification.

The problem isn't that you are not working hard enough; rather, it's that you agreed to do the task by tomorrow. Instead of committing to something unrealistic, *just shut up*. Understand your time commitments and instead say you will get it done by the end of the week.

I have found that the problem with most business owners is that they are working too hard. For these people, the way to fix the equation is to just shut up. Quit making promises you can't keep.

Like most advice, this is easier said than done. In my case, I needed to do work on both sides of the equation.

I committed to balancing what I say with what I do by creating the following guidelines for myself:

1. Always show up ten minutes early to a meeting. Don't walk in late or even right on time looking rushed.
2. End your meetings on time, too, regardless of whether you are finished or not. Most of the time, your commitment to timeliness is more important than what you are discussing at that moment in a meeting.
3. Give yourself plenty of time to do your work so you don't miss deadlines. Don't be afraid to say "no" or push back if you don't think you can finish something on time.
4. If you miss a deadline, don't make excuses—say it like it is! "I failed to meet the deadline."

Stop overpromising your time. Don't tell someone you can be there, do that, help them, or finish that project when there is no possible way to make it happen. Just stop.

People within your organization need to know they can count on you. They need to be able to trust you. They are unable to do so if you continue to make commitments that you don't keep. You say you're going to be somewhere, and you show up late. You say you will have something completed, and you don't. The easiest way to fix Accountability Equations is to stop saying it—only promise what you are 100 percent sure you are going to be able to accomplish.

Lead by example and show people what accountability looks like. If you fail, fall on your sword and admit it. Admitting when you make a mistake is harder than it sounds since business owners have a lot of pride. It might not seem like a good idea for leaders to admit that they are not infallible, but the long-term results of openly admitting failure are part of building an accountable culture where people on your team admit mistakes freely instead of covering them up. As a leader, admitting a mistake takes courage and is powerful.

STOP DREAM-VOMITING

I am an out-loud dreamer. In my early days as a leader, I would get excited about my latest ideas and tell my team immediately about all the great things we *might* do in the future. While communicating your vision is important, blabbing every idea that pops into your head can be overwhelming and confusing to your team, no matter how wonderful you think your ideas are.

> **Stop dream-vomiting on your team. People get tired of talk and want action. Say less, but when you do say something, mean it. This is how you earn people's trust.**

I have noticed that some business owners use their position in the company as a way to stand on a pulpit and give long, drawn-out, rambling speeches. They have an audience who is paid to listen. While their team has no choice but to listen, after a while, their eyes glaze over. They are hearing, but are they really listening?

We have all met quiet leaders who listen and watch. They don't say much, but when they do, they command the attention of everyone in the room, and you know what they are saying will be profound and backed by action. Strive to be more like that type of leader.

> *As a leader, your communication style needs to be strategic and measured.*

You may find that some members on the team can brainstorm with you, but in these cases, make it clear before you open your mouth that this is a brainstorming session only and not the launch of a new strategy.

AT THE END OF THE DAY

The hardest thing to change is ourselves, and that is usually what is holding us back. My dad said that if you want to win in business, you have to wake up earlier than your competition. He wasn't talking about the time you wake up in the morning in the literal sense but instead about how hard you are willing to work. Are you willing to work harder and do things that your competition won't? Are you willing to follow through on *the promises you made to yourself*, rather than just ones you made to others?

Most people lack the discipline to run a business well. It is much easier to be held accountable when you report to a boss and know there is a potential for termination if something doesn't get done. Some people have enough accountability to start a business, but once it starts making enough money to maintain their lifestyle, they start slacking off. Growing a company isn't a sprint; it's a marathon and requires stamina.

Look deeply at yourself and ask whether you are setting the right example for your team. Is your kitchen clean, or are there some lumps of butter and crumbs on the counter?

END OF CHAPTER CHECKLIST

Do an honest assessment of your own accountability by answering the following questions:

- ❏ Am **I** late to meetings?
- ❏ Do **my** meetings end on time?
- ❏ Do **I** cancel or fail to show up to 1-2-1 meetings with my team?
- ❏ Do **I** miss my deadlines?

- ❏ Do I overcommit to doing things and then fail to meet my promises to my team and customers?
- ❏ Do I bring up ideas and innovative solutions to my team and then fail to follow through with time and resources to implement them?
- ❏ Do I start implementing ideas, lose passion, and then switch to the next great idea?
- ❏ When I am late or miss deadlines, do I give some excuse to minimize my lack of accountability?

If you answered yes to any of these questions, you have some work to do to increase your level of accountability.

4

Jack and Shirley

My gateway book that created my obsession with business culture was *Pour Your Heart into It* by Howard Schultz. He writes about his love for Starbucks as if the company were another woman in his life. You could take the word *Starbucks* out of most of the book's passages and replace it with a random woman's name, like Becky, and the sentence would sound like part of a love story.

The sign of a good business owner is when your company becomes your passion. But when your passion is your business, what does that mean for your spouse or significant other?

START-UPS ARE FAMILY AFFAIRS

Part of getting in the position to scale your company is making sure you have support in your personal life. Owning your own business can cause friction in your personal relationships. After I bought the company from my dad, he came to the company Christmas party as a guest with my mom. I gave a speech in front of the staff and drivers and recognized him for all his hard work and sacrifices to get 3 Men Movers off the ground. It was an impassioned speech, and I went back to my seat thinking, *Nailed it!*

After I sat down, he leaned over and angrily told me to never talk about the hard work and sacrifices he made unless I mentioned "your mother." "He" didn't start 3 Men Movers; "he" wasn't the founder—it was both of them. "She was right there with me the whole way, and if it wasn't for her support, I never would have gotten the business off the ground," he said.

While she never had an official position with the company, her support for my dad and his vision was unwavering.

HOW IT ALL STARTED

The story of how 3 Men Movers came about is a love story that started way back in the 1970s with my dad, John Fischer, better known as Jack. Jack was from a small town in Illinois. In his early thirties, he was a bachelor, and most nights he went out drinking, dancing, and playing pool. He got into barroom brawls, usually getting thrown out. He claimed that he never started a fight, but he never backed down from one either.

Jack was a rebel without a cause, until one day, when he met and fell in love with Shirley Ellen Russell. At the time, Shirley was divorced with four teenage kids. Suddenly, he had four teenage "causes" who went through three gallons of milk and two loaves of bread in a single weekend, and soon there was a baby, me, on the way.

Jack had drifted from job to job doing mostly blue-collar work in factories and agricultural fields and on assembly lines and construction crews. When he got married, he knew he had to put down his pool cue, cut his hair, stop job drifting, and get serious about making ends meet. Having no college education, the closest Jack could get to a career was to become a Kirby vacuum cleaner salesman. He bought himself a three-piece suit and hit the road selling vacuum cleaners.

Jack became phenomenally successful at selling Kirby vacuum cleaners and opened up a distributorship in his hometown. He hired a small army of vacuum cleaner salespeople to grow his company. At one time, he had the highest-performing territory in the Midwest. He loved being an entrepreneur and clearly had a knack for business and sales.

My first business memories are from this time. I accompanied him to the sales meetings when I was four years old, and he would place me on top of the desk where I would sing, "I've got that good ole Kirby spirit up in my heart, up in my heart." I remember the groovy 1970s shag carpet in his office and the smell of cigarettes and coffee. It was like a scene from *Glengarry Glen Ross*.

By the early 1980s, high interest rates had burst the agricultural speculative bubble in our area, and Illinois went through a recession. People could not get credit to finance the purchase of an expensive Kirby vacuum cleaner. The Kirby business began to fail, and Jack needed to make a change.

Jack decided that we should pick up and move to Texas, which Shirley's conservative family was not happy about. First, she had divorced her first husband, then she had married the town's wild man, and if that weren't enough of a shock, now she was going to take off across the country with him to a big city with no real plan and little money. This was during a time before cell phones, cheap flights, and the Internet—the world was a bigger place back then. A move across the country might as well have been a move across the planet, especially when you were poor and couldn't afford long-distance phone bills and expensive flights home.

In 1982, Jack drove down to Houston, Texas, to set up a new life for us. Houston was booming at the time. He found an apartment, and six months later sent for Shirley and me to join him. At that time, my siblings were all grown up and living on their own, and I was the last kid left at home. We didn't have money to hire movers, so Shirley traded her big Midwestern Crown Victoria four-door sedan for a Texas-style 1978 Ford F-150 truck, which was novel in Illinois during the 1980s. The truck was green with a yellow stripe down the center and didn't have air-conditioning, so we rode around with the radio up and the windows down. We drove out of town with our two cats in the cab and tons of boxes covered in plastic in the bed of the truck, looking much like the Beverly Hillbillies, but instead of heading west to California, we turned south on the interstate toward Texas.

A BRAVE NEW WORLD

Jack had landed in Houston just in time for the savings and loan crisis, which, at the time, created the greatest banking collapse since the Great Depression in 1929, and the epicenter of this economic disaster was our new home, Texas.

Texas was reeling from a drop in oil prices, high vacancy, unemployment, and home foreclosures. It seemed bad luck was following us. Jack lacked a college education to compete in the job market against young, college-educated job hunters. He was in his late forties and still hadn't been able find some type of work to provide a decent living for his family. Houston's glittering promise lost its luster. Jack and Shirley were getting desperate.

Shirley was able to find a job as a desk assistant at the city library, making minimum wage. For a while, she was the sole breadwinner. She never complained, waking early to catch the METRO bus to and from work while Jack took the only car to look for a job. They were barely making ends meet.

Each week, Shirley entered a lottery the public library ran to determine who would be picked to work at one of the few libraries open on Sundays: Success meant she was paid time and a half, money we desperately needed. Frequently, she worked seven days a week.

Jack tried everything to make money. He went from selling cigarette vending machines to buying shrimp off the docks in Galveston and then driving back to Houston and selling the shrimp from a stand he would set up on the side of the road. When I wasn't at school, I usually was dragged around in our old pickup truck while he tried to make some cash. I would sit next to the truck all summer removing shrimp heads for customers who would pay more per pound if they didn't have to do the shelling themselves. I was quite chuffed with myself because I learned to quickly chuck two heads at once, one in each hand.

This period was the darkest time for our family. Jack felt horrible about not being able to provide the life he wanted for us. He was from an era when supporting your family was considered a man's primary job, and he felt like a failure. He hated that Shirley had to work so hard and dreamed of a day when she could stay at home and work on her art. She had aspirations of being an artist, and he encouraged her, but usually she returned home from work exhausted and too tired to paint.

Shirley learned that she could make a little more money if she took a position driving the bookmobile for Harris County. The bookmobile was a huge semi that housed a mini-library, which was driven out to new communities in the suburbs of Houston that didn't yet have a library. To qualify for this position, Shirley needed a CDL license, so she enrolled in trucking school.

During this time, Jack started a company that built unfinished bunk beds and sold them to local furniture stores. He did most of the work on his own, except for occasionally hiring extra help in busy times. He had a small warehouse, again with no air-conditioning, and created a small, makeshift assembly line to produce the beds quickly out of cheap yellow pine, which he marketed as "hand-sanded." The real reason they were hand-sanded was because he couldn't afford a power sander. Unfortunately, the business eventually went bust.

Jack was left with a run-down delivery truck and a stack of bills. Rich people go bankrupt, while poor people just go broke. Bankruptcy is a luxury that comes with lawyers who swoop in to help you disentangle yourself from debt by negotiating on your behalf. Broke just left you flat on your ass and desperate.

Our future looked bleak. At age fifty, Jack was at the end of his rope. He had dragged his wife and young child away from their small town and family ties. Now they were in a strange, big city and without money. It does something to a man's psyche when he is unable to support his family. He became depressed and despondent, but Shirley's support and loyalty never wavered—she was the family's rock. Jack could have quit his dreams of owning a business and gotten a minimum-wage job, but he wanted to get his family out of living paycheck to paycheck, and he knew getting a low-paying job would never put us in a position of financial security. He was willing to take short-term risks to achieve his long-term goals.

In 1985, Jack decided to put the delivery truck left over from the furniture manufacturing company to work. He put an ad in a local advertising publication for furniture moving services. It was something he was going to do for a few months until he could figure out something better to do. At age fifty, Jack started moving furniture.

During this time, the moving industry was unregulated, so you didn't need a license to operate. Jack showed up to the customers' houses on time and in uniform and gave excellent service. Pretty soon he began to get referrals.

Jack came up with the name 3 Men Movers, not because he started the company with two other guys, but because he wanted the company's listing to show up first in the Yellow Pages phone book. The number "3" put us as the first mover listed, even before ABC Moving.

A few years later, we saved our money and were finally able to move out of our low-income apartment and into a starter home, which we bought from foreclosure for $27,000. We moved out of the apartment and into the suburbs. It was a tiny house, but it had three bedrooms, giving our new company an office of its own in the third bedroom.

As the moving business continued to grow, Jack bought his first big gooseneck trailer. He parked a beast of a truck in front of our little house, but he could not figure out how to unhook the trailer from the power unit tractor part. We watched him through the front window as he became impatient, rubbing his eyes and cursing as he jerked the equipment around. He twisted the crank, then got into the truck and pulled it forward, then got back out and did it all over again, but the trailer stubbornly wouldn't disconnect. He began growling and rubbing his eyes. It wasn't working—the hitch was stuck.

Shirley went outside and asked him if he needed help. Frustrated, he shooed her away and continued to try to release the trailer. Shirley went into the house, and after a few hours of watching him struggle, she returned, grabbed the hitch crank with her tiny hands, rotated the crank until it was in the right position, jumped into the tractor, started it up, and then pulled it carefully away from the trailer. The CDL training from driving the bookmobile came in handy. After she unhooked the trailer, she calmly climbed down and without a word handed the keys to Jack, then walked back into the house. He stood quietly and stared at her as she disappeared inside.

THE STRENGTH OF TRIANGLES

For an owner, a business can be like a third person in your relationship. Hopefully, you will be lucky to raise some start-up capital in the beginning, but if you are bootstrapping your company, you may need not only mental support but also a partner who is willing to provide the steady income in the first few years while your company ramps up. Until a business gets established, the income from a spouse with a steady job can mean the difference between feast or famine.

And then there is the whole work-life balance thing people talk about. It cracks me up when friends of mine say that they want to quit their corporate jobs and start a business so they can set their hours and have more free time. That can happen someday, but in the beginning, it is an all-out, nonstop effort to get things off the ground, especially if you have limited resources. When you have a corporate job, you worry about your paycheck. When you own your own business, you worry about *everyone's* paycheck. When you have a corporate job, you get to leave work at work. When you own your own business, you carry the stress around with you like a huge weight.

Owning your own business can be all-encompassing and leave a spouse feeling lonely. If you are starting a business, discuss the toll it will take on your relationship and what sacrifices both of you will be willing to take for the business. Also, discuss what boundaries you are willing to set to protect your family time.

It isn't always wise or recommended for a spouse to give blind loyalty and support. Sometimes, if a business is failing, you have to cut your losses. However, it is hard to grow a successful business without the support of your significant other and your family. While this book can help you find a better work-life balance, as a business owner, you are always "on," and it takes a special kind of person who can accept that commitment in your life.

Jack—my dad—always knew that Shirley—my mother—had his back. Even during hard times, they were a team: Not only did they dream of a better future; they dreamed of that future better together.

END OF CHAPTER CHECKLIST

Conversations to have with your significant other to better manage the third wheel in your relationship:

- ❏ Do we need boundaries set around cell phone usage? Example: A date night with the cell phone turned off? After 7 PM? On the weekends? During vacations?
- ❏ Where are we financially? If the business starts losing money, how long are we committed to supporting it? Is there a line when the support stops, and if so, where is that line?
- ❏ What is the eventual exit plan? What happens to the business if I die or get sick?
- ❏ What processes do we have set up to be able to unhook from the business during the weekends and holidays and enjoy together time?
- ❏ Do I bring stress home after work, and is it affecting our personal life?
- ❏ Is the risk and additional stress of business ownership worth it?

5

Zero Fucks

Leadership is a balancing act. Great leaders need buy-in to reach their goals, so being liked is important. However, great leaders are not consumed with the need to be liked to the point that it affects their decision-making.

Fear of rejection can hinder your ability to lead. Rejection comes in many different forms and starts from the time we are children, from not being accepted on the playground or having a parent who rejects us, all the way to having a spouse file for divorce. Rejection is painful. Any form of rejection can take an enormous toll on your life. Most of us make decisions on how we navigate life based on rejection avoidance.

In leadership, rejection comes with the job.

THE NEED FOR ACCEPTANCE

Humans are tribal creatures because within the tribe there is safety. Rejection from the tribe could mean death for early humans. In a group, they received protection from predators and received nourishment by being able to surround and kill animals and gather food in groups.

Women giving birth and raising children alone were at significant risk, but within a group, they received protection during this vulnerable time. Could this be why studies show that women seek to be accepted and liked more so than men?

Ostracism from the tribe was a death sentence to our ancestors; with acceptance from your tribe came increased rates of survival.

Deciding to become a leader goes against our most primal fear: rejection. Being a follower within a tribe helps ensure your survival. You align with the tribe. Being a leader and pushing against the status quo could be detrimental to your survival. What if the group rejects your ideas? What if people decide to leave and abandon you?

MAKING THE TOUGH DECISIONS

As a leader, one of your most important jobs is to make tough decisions. Fear of making unpopular decisions can stunt your company's growth. It is not always possible or recommended to seek out the entire company to get a majority vote when making major decisions. It is nice to live in a democratic country, but owning a democratic company can cause you to not keep pace with the ever-changing market conditions. Seeking buy-in from all employees can cripple a company because, in the marketplace, decisions need to be made constantly and quickly. Usually, there is no time to vote for each decision that needs to be made.

Often, individuals are motivated by self-interest. When making big decisions, it is important to get feedback from your employees and your leadership team, but the final decision should be made by you. Unlike the citizens of a country, people on your team can and do leave when they disagree with the direction of a company. Also unlike a nation's citizens, employees won't wait around for the next election. Losing people because they don't accept your vision is a risk, but a necessary one.

My dad wanted to be accepted and liked, but he gave "zero fucks" if he felt he was right, even if you didn't like him because of it. When he sold the company, he retired and moved to Gilchrist, Texas, a coastal community, to be by the water. He built my mother a little art studio behind their home so she could finally become the artist she was meant to be. My dad was no longer a businessman, so he let his hair grow long again and tried to settle into retirement, but he remained a leader.

In the afternoon, he would drive down to the local bar, The Ship's Wheel, and have a drink, and when he would hear some of the bigoted men at the bar saying derogatory things about Blacks and gays, he would speak up. The bar patrons would usually write him off as being an old hippie.

Soon, when he would enter the bar, the locals would say, "Here comes the [N-word] lover and fag**t lover." My dad was in his eighties and too old to punch the guy out, but he did not shrink away; instead, he walked right in with his chest stuck out and replied, "You're goddamn right I am!"

Good leaders are unafraid to express their beliefs.

SPEED BUMPS

In the first few years of starting the moving business, my dad put an ad in the paper to hire "truck drivers." He didn't realize that there is a difference between a mover who also drives a truck and a truck driver. A truck driver focuses on driving a truck, usually an 18-wheeler, on long-haul, solitary routes. A trucker backs up to warehouse loading docks, and warehouse workers take the load on and off his truck. He doesn't touch the load. A mover, on the other hand, not only drives a truck but is also a leader who manages a crew and has customer service skills. He is also willing to do the manual labor of loading the truck. To most people, this difference might seem insignificant; however, to a trucker, this is a big deal. Truckers are not movers.

The ad was placed while we were still in a recession during the 1980s, and there was a huge response from over one hundred desperate truckers looking for work. Instead of picking one or two guys to interview, my dad saw the response from so many as an opportunity. Wanting to help these men in a larger way, he had devised a way to get all of them work. Remembering his Kirby vacuum cleaner days of having an army of commissioned salespeople, he thought that he could get these unemployed men motivated to go out and market 3 Men Movers. The truckers could find customers who wanted to move by visiting local apartment complexes, networking, and handing out business cards, and when they were able to get the jobs, they could use his truck and split the profit.

Basically, he would take unemployed men and help them learn to market and sell the moving services so they could get work for themselves. He thought they would be excited to be able to be in control of their destiny. Instead of being unemployed and waiting at home for a job, they could create their own revenue stream. He invited everyone who inquired about the job to a local diner one Saturday morning to hear his pitch. Over one hundred men planned to show up, and my dad made arrangements ahead of time to section off an area of the restaurant.

I was there when the men started showing up. We had little money, but my dad bought them all coffee. The men reminded me of guys you would expect at a 1980s rock concert: Harley-Davidson riders—the real deal, not accountants riding on weekends—blue jeans, long hair, and tattoos. The room filled up with about seventy tough-looking truckers, and my dad went to the front of the room and then laid out his idea of how they could all be partners and make money. They listened intently, but when it began to dawn on them that my dad didn't have jobs for everyone, they got upset. One guy started shouting that my dad "wasted my fucking time." Another guy threw his cup of coffee toward the front of the room as he got up and left. Pretty soon everyone was grumbling, and I could hear the sound of chairs scooting across the tile floor as they stood up to leave. When everyone had left, my dad paid the bill and drove us home in silence.

The next day he was on to his next big idea. Obstacles that got in the way of his goals were like speed bumps in the road—they slowed him down momentarily, but he kept on moving.

TOUGHENED UP

As a child I was sickly, scrawny, and pasty white. I was timid and cried when little things scared me. My dad worked hard at trying to toughen me up. When I was in school, rejection and the need for acceptance was a powerful motivator. I realize my need to be liked is a normal human emotion, which initially hurt me as a leader. In the beginning, I feared rejection, and that fear prevented me from making decisions that I knew were in the best interest of the company. I didn't want people to be upset with me.

I would send out group emails, rather than talking with one person face-to-face, because I was too afraid to confront someone directly. If I had one employee who was habitually late for meetings and nine others who were always on time, I would send an email out to all ten employees: "Everyone, please make sure that we are on time to the team meetings so we can finish on time." I didn't want to make waves and feared rejection, so I took a general, ineffective approach instead of a direct approach. My attempt of trying to smooth things over prevented me from having critical conversations with employees who needed feedback to grow. It wasn't kind to keep someone in the dark about their performance because of my fear of having a critical conversation and my desire to be liked. It also wasn't kind to send an email out reminding nine people to be on time when they never had an issue with timeliness.

Once, we hired a receptionist who seemed kindhearted and interviewed well, but shortly after we hired her, her behavior changed. One day she was well put-together, and the next day she looked disheveled. Then, she began missing work.

One Saturday I arrived at the office to find her hunched over at the receptionist desk, wrapped in a blanket. I thought maybe she had a cold or the flu. After speaking with her manager, I found out that several years ago her son was murdered during a carjacking.

Being a mother, I was horrified at what had happened to this woman. Days passed into weeks, and weeks passed into months. Her behavior didn't improve. She was suffering from depression. Her behavior began to hurt our business.

I asked a mentor for advice and was told that at some point she needed to "get over it" and "do her job." He asked me if I was running a business or a charity. I said, "A business." He responded, "If you want to give money to a charity, that is fine, but stop running your business like one."

I knew as a mother that there are some things you just don't "get over," and your son's murder is one of them. Weeks passed, and her job performance continued to suffer. My empathy for her took away all objectivity and rendered me powerless in addressing the situation. I had to hire another person to take up the slack that she created. If I fired her, it would be the right thing for the company, but to me would be unethical given her suffering. Her manager spoke to her often, encouraging her to get professional help for her depression. After months passed, I finally decided that I'd had enough and called her in to my office. Not only was I worried about her; I was also worried about the tone I would set throughout the company if I let her go. Would my people think I was heartless?

Finally, I told her that I could not keep her employed if she didn't show up to work. She began to cry and acknowledged that she was depressed and needed help. I eventually had to fire her, and that was the catalyst she needed to seek out professional help for her depression.

Later, my team told me that, while they felt bad for her, too, they could not understand why I hadn't fired her sooner. She was affecting the success of the entire company, and that had the potential to hurt many lives if she prevented the company from being profitable. It was a tough decision that I put off making for too long because I was afraid of hurting her and appearing insensitive to my team.

As a business owner, part of your job is deciding between taking actions that negatively affect an employee or a department and taking actions that negatively impact the overall success of the company—always make a decision based on what is best for the entire organization. When I make a decision with this rule in mind, the decision always works out. When I have gone against this rule, I usually regret my decision.

I learned from my father that, as a leader, you have to make unpopular decisions and have uncomfortable conversations that might cause people to reject you. It would be nice to sail through life with everyone loving you, but it isn't realistic, especially if you are in a leadership role.

Think of yourself as a product: a niche product. Not everyone will like you, and that is okay.

END OF CHAPTER CHECKLIST

- ❏ Is my need for acceptance, "to be liked," holding me back from having crucial conversations with people on my team?
- ❏ Am I holding back on making a tough decision because I am afraid of how one person might feel, instead of looking at the big picture and how this could have a negative effect on the entire company?
- ❏ Do I take a general approach with an email to a group, or a general announcement, because I am afraid to have a direct conversation with an individual?
- ❏ Does my attempt to be seen as "nice" prevent me from being an effective leader?

END OF PART 1 CHECKLIST

- ☐ I have thought about and understand what gives my life purpose and meaning.
- ☐ I am ready to make changes for the long-term strategic benefits of my business.
- ☐ I understand that these changes might have short-term negative consequences.
- ☐ I have thought about the fears I have that might be preventing me from changing:

    Fear of rejection
    Fear of failure
    Fear of the unknown

- ☐ Is my comfort lifestyle creating status-quo behavior? Am I settling? Is *good enough* preventing me from becoming *great*?
- ☐ I have looked in the mirror and given myself an honest evaluation of my own accountability.
- ☐ I have decided what personal actions I will take to improve my own accountability. *Is my kitchen clean?*
- ☐ I will make the commitment to lead by example by becoming more accountable to myself and my team.
- ☐ I will lead better by keeping my mouth shut and not overpromising, and working harder to deliver on what I do promise.
- ☐ I have discussed my business commitments with my significant other and have his or her support. We have set boundaries around personal time and work time.
- ☐ I will give *zero fucks* about doing things that people won't like if I know, in my heart, it is what is right for the success of the company.
- ☐ I will not put off unpopular decisions out of fear if I know that it is the right path forward.
- ☐ I have identified a person on my team who I have been procrastinating having a difficult conversation with, and I have scheduled a meeting with that person.

- ❑ I am ready to take action on the one decision that I need to make, that I know is right, that I am not doing because I am afraid.
- ❑ I am a *niche product*, and not everyone has to like me, and that is okay.

Note to Reader: So here you are! Congratulations, you finished the first section of *The Growth Paradox*. It is important to start with a bunch of psychology stuff to ensure you personally have the mental tools it takes to grow a company. I promise you that the rest of the book will contain tactical information, but to get there, you must be in the right mindset. By now, you should have thought about:

- ❑ your personal "why,"
- ❑ your fear of failure that might be preventing you from taking actions that will ultimately grow your company,
- ❑ your own accountability,
- ❑ your family support system,
- ❑ your need to be liked and its role in preventing you from making unpopular decisions.

As a business owner, you are ready for the next step.

A company that is ready for rapid growth must start with a good foundation. In Part 2, you will learn how to create that foundation.

PART 2

Building a Skyscraper?
Start Digging!

6

Begin with the End

Most business books start by telling you to write a *mission statement*. There is a reason everyone starts with this task: You must have the purpose for your organization written in a succinct manner so that everyone on your team can quickly get on the same page. This mission statement should be your *Why*: Why is everyone showing up to work, day after day?

Your mission statement should be your end game, what your company hopes to ultimately accomplish.

CHOOSE YOUR MISSION WISELY

When I first started, I was out to prove the bankers, who rejected my loan request, wrong. I was confident that I knew what I was doing: I was going to grow the business. As the leader of the company, I focused my team on *growth*. Our mission statement was to be the biggest moving company in Texas. But the more we focused on growth, the more we lost sight of creating value for our customers. We lost sight of the reason we were in business.

Our reason for being in business was straightforward: to help people on their move day. When we focused on growth, we became overly concerned with adding the next thousand customers instead of helping the individual customer who was standing in front of us. *We became intoxicated by being the biggest, while we lost focus on being the best.*

We were trying so hard to win big that we were losing the moment, and our moment is helping that special customer we are servicing today: Janis Wilkinson, who recently went through a divorce and is feeling overwhelmed, sad, stressed, and wondering how she is going to handle life on her own; Jason Castillo, who just got a promotion and a raise and is excited to move into a nicer apartment but needs help with his packing because of his long work hours; the Nelson family, who are downsizing after selling their large home in the suburbs and are moving into town after helping their last kid move off to college; Sharon Martinez, who is her mother's caretaker and had the responsibility for arranging her mother's move from the home she lived in for over forty years to assisted living.

We lost focus on the customers as individuals and became consumed with the big numbers. We focused on cutting a percentage here and increasing a percentage there to make a little more on the bottom line. When we realized that we were losing our competitive edge on what always had been our advantage, award-winning customer service, we had to take inventory of who we were, who we wanted to be, and why we were in business in the first place.

We decided to update our mission statement: *To create loyal fans one move at a time.*

We didn't want "customer satisfaction" in the way that a McDonald's hamburger will satisfy your hunger—the food might not taste great, but you won't be hungry after you eat it. We wanted to create a fan base. To do that, we had to go beyond satisfying our customers. We had to knock our customers' socks off with each interaction.

We emphasized *One Move at a Time* to remind us to slow down and win the moment with each customer. From then on, when we made decisions in the office, we could "check" our decisions by asking, "Is this going to create a loyal fan?"

> ***A simple change to your mission statement, communicated clearly to your team, will help you refocus on what is truly important.***

Ask yourself why you are in business. Remember Viktor Frankl's claim that the meaning of life is *to find a purpose*. Finding your company's purpose is just as important as uncovering your personal mission. A well-written mission statement gives your team purpose. You are asking your team to dedicate years of their lives to your company and its mission, so it is important to make the mission worthwhile.

Money and growth for the sake of being "big" isn't enough of a purpose for employees. If they show up to work just for the money, then they will leave you if someone offers them a dollar more an hour at a company down the street. Money should be the result of everyone accomplishing their mission.

TAKE THE MONEY OUT OF YOUR MISSION

When I started out, Mike Rydin, one of my mentors who started a successful construction software company, told me to stop focusing on the money. I thought, *Easy for you to say, Mr. Millionaire, when your company is phenomenally successful and practically printing cash.* At the time, I wasn't making much in profits. Most of the money I made, after I wrote the monthly check to my parents, was reinvested in the company to build infrastructure for growth. I did an internal eye roll and thought, *He doesn't get it because he doesn't have to worry about making money.*

I was raised to always think about money because there was a huge shortage of it throughout my childhood. It wasn't until years later that I realized that Mike was right. It isn't that making money is not important or satisfying, but it is hard to get you or your team rallied around making the company richer. Helping your customers and your team are more purposeful goals to focus on.

Money does help you keep track of whether you are successful at achieving your mission. Gross revenue is an indication of whether your customers value you and your business's products and services enough to pay for them. Profits indicate if you are running your business efficiently. If your mission is about creating value for your customers and your business structure is set up to be profitable, then if you achieve your mission, the results should equal profits.

Create a mission statement if you don't already have one. If you already have a mission statement, ask yourself if it is your *Why*. Does it resonate enough with your team to give them a purpose in their daily work? It's important for there to be significant purpose in our work. After all, we spend over one-third of our adult lives working. Purpose in our work gives us meaning in our lives.

END OF CHAPTER CHECKLIST

- ❑ Does my company have a written mission statement?
- ❑ Does my company's mission statement resonate with my team and give them purpose?
- ❑ Is the mission statement shared with everyone in the company?
- ❑ Do people have it memorized? (Hint, make it easy to memorize! Short and memorable.)
- ❑ Do we refer to the mission statement when my team discusses major decisions to ensure it aligns with our mission?

I ask business owners, "What is your mission statement?" They respond, "Oh, I have one of those. I can't remember what it is, but it is written down somewhere."

Remember, for a mission statement to be purposeful, don't just paint it on a wall or print it in an employee handbook and then ignore it. Your mission statement is a tool that should be used often in the day-to-day running of your business. Everyone on your team should know it by heart, and you should be referring to it weekly to run your business. If it doesn't naturally come out in conversations when you are trying to make decisions, then you don't have a mission statement.

A mission statement is the cornerstone that gives your team guidance when making tough decisions.

7

Fail to Plan, Plan to Fail

Years ago, I read a novel about a rural couple who added a room to their house every time they added an offspring. They ended up having eight kids, and the house became a Frankenstein house—a sprawling, hodgepodge monstrosity of disconnected rooms. If the couple understood their need for more rooms before they started having kids, they could have sat down and carefully designed the home in the beginning and then added rooms in stages over time in a thoughtful manner.

Your plan is to grow your company. Let's take for granted that you will be successful. Therefore, you should start planning an infrastructure to handle your business's future growth *now*. You will need to get your people and processes in place to handle the company you will become in three to five years. Business owners often fail because they are too "in the moment." They are focused on what their company needs right now, and when you run a growing company that way, you will always be trying to build an infrastructure to catch up with your growth. You will always be behind growth, which will make your decisions reactionary. Preplanning your business needs will ensure that growth is not hindered in order for your infrastructure to catch up.

Some businesses are structured like that sprawling, unorganized house. A business may be started by a *solopreneur* (a single-person company), a person with an idea. In the beginning, that person wears many hats. When the business owner has too much work to handle on their own, they hire another person to do more of what they are doing, which is a bit of everything. That person usually becomes the "mini-me" of the owner and focuses on the tasks the owner doesn't have time to do, isn't good at doing, or maybe just doesn't want to do. Maybe this person is focused on administrative tasks while the owner is out generating more sales, or vice versa.

As the business expands and has more needs, more people are added, like the rooms in the unplanned house. You just slap on another room without much planning. Most companies in this phase are usually not focused on building their infrastructure. Most are focused on either trying to get more business or, if they are lucky, trying to keep up with the business they have. *Reactionary hiring* occurs when people are hired as solutions to problems instead of being part of a long-term strategic plan. Sometimes the problems can be solved with better processes, new software, upgrading your existing team with training, or replacing people who are unable to handle growth.

People tend to grow their companies the opposite way they should. They grow their revenue, then rush to put the infrastructure in place to keep up with the demand for their products and services. This puts the company in crisis mode as it tries to keep up with growth. It is difficult to grow a multimillion-dollar company without first creating a solid infrastructure that can handle the customers' demands.

DON'T HIRE SOMEONE FOR TODAY'S JOB—INSTEAD, HIRE UP

Companies also hire the opposite way they should. For example, when a business owner is running a one million–dollar company and they hire someone to run their Accounting department, they will put an ad out looking for an accountant who can manage the books for a one million–dollar company. Seems logical, right? Often, they will even accept someone who has run the books for a smaller company and is looking for a "promotion" by moving to a larger company. Let them get their work experience somewhere else. You want someone who can do the books for a $3–5 million company and brings their previous experience to help you, because that is the size of the company you are growing toward becoming. If you hire down, meaning you hire someone who does not have the experience working at the size and complexity of the company you want to be, you will outgrow this new hire quickly and will need to find their replacement or train them to be the person that can meet the demands of your growing company.

If you have people on your team who don't have the necessary training and experience, they will be overwhelmed, and mistakes will happen. When mistakes happen, the owner will become the office asshole, exerting total control to prevent future mistakes. This becomes a self-fulfilling prophecy. The owner will stop working on strategy and will start working in the business doing menial work. As the company continues to grow, the owner, now working on the day-to-day running of the business to prevent mistakes, will lose focus on strategic hiring and will instead make reactionary hires to quickly put bodies in seats—and, again, more mistakes will happen. This type of hiring can put the owner and the company into a downward spiral of costly mistakes, bad hires, and a loss of strategic goals that will stagnate the company growth trajectory.

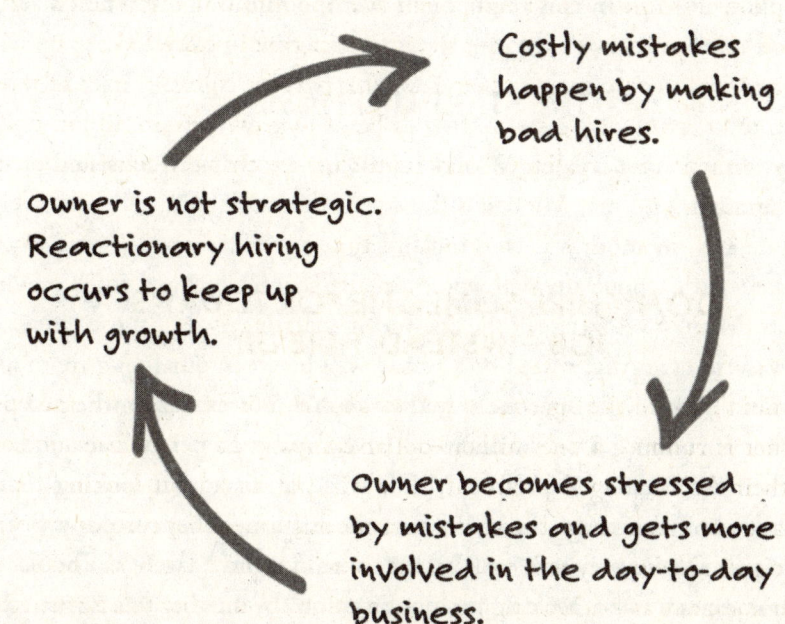

THE HAMSTER WHEEL OF NONSTRATEGIC THINKING

When my company was growing, I went through a period of hiring accountants who were underqualified. I was hiring people who could barely handle the position, and we kept outgrowing them. Part of the reason was that I wasn't willing to take the financial hit to hire someone who could run the books of a large company. The result was years of late financial reports, costly accounting mistakes, and a ton of stress. I finally bit the bullet and hired someone who asked for about 20 percent more than what I thought I should have paid—and it was one of the best decisions I ever made. Kathryn Cheung came in with years of experience and knew exactly what to do. Unlike her predecessors, who were completely overwhelmed with the work, she handled the job with ease. She came in and told me what I needed to do to get my books cleaned up. You know you hired the right person for the job when they can tell you what needs to be done instead of looking at you to tell them what they need to do.

Hire someone from the type of company you want to be in five years who already knows how to put structures and processes in place that you may not have currently. *Hire someone who can come in and tell you what you need to do, not someone whom you need to tell what to do.* If you do not hire up, you will always be in catch-up mode. That bookkeeper you just hired who understands how to run a million-dollar company might be in over their head in just a few years.

THE START-UP PHASE

When we first started 3 Men Movers in 1985, the company consisted of my dad, my mother, and me. My dad did most of the work because I was twelve at the time and my mom was working full-time at the library. When I would come home from school, my dad would usually still be out on a truck moving customers. My job was to check the answering machine, one of those old kinds with a cassette tape, that rested on the bar area between our living room and dining room in our little apartment and write down messages on the notepad we kept by the phone. After I finished, I would call each person back and ask them about their upcoming move. My dad had a script with pricing that I was supposed to go over with each customer. Sometimes they would say, "You sound so young—how old are you?" And I would reply, "Twelve." The use of child labor seemed to bother no one since customers went ahead and scheduled their move anyway.

My mother was in charge of all the marketing and most of the administrative work. This was before computers, so she would create designs for the flyers and business cards by hand. She also helped Dad after work with his accounting and wrote checks to make sure the bills were paid. Many small businesses start off with this "all-hands-on-deck" approach. The "all-hands-on-deck" structure, or actually lack of structure, works fine for a start-up with limited resources, but in order to grow, you have to begin to delineate job duties and put formal processes in place.

By the time I returned to the company in my late twenties, there were five people working in the office and fifteen crews in the field. The structure looked like the Start-Up Phase diagram below. It was still running in much the same way it did when I was a kid, which prevented the company from scaling. My dad was still the boss, but instead of my mom and me supporting him, we were replaced by six helpers. This is sometimes referred to as the Chief-with-Many-Helpers Model: The chief did the bossing, and then everyone did a bit of everything, but usually they focused on what they did best. Marketing/sales tended to be done by people who liked to talk to people, and we had some "back office"

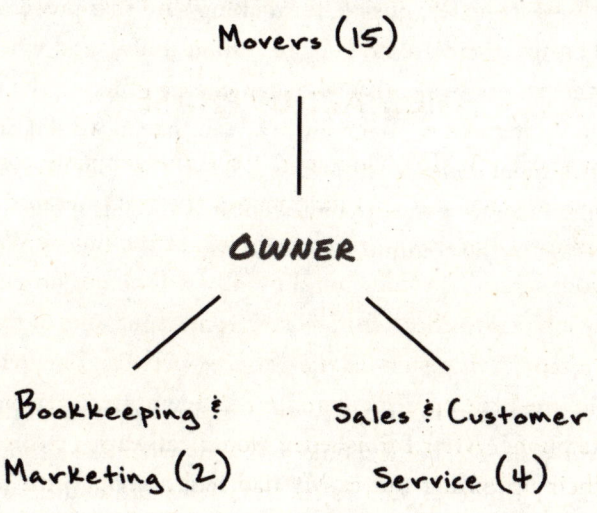

THE START-UP PHASE:
Owner (the Chief) managing everything and everyone.

people who took payments, handled claims, and managed the books. At that time, nobody was specialized in a particular field.

When there are only a handful of people working with you, this type of structure works fine and is efficient, so long as the chief is always around barking orders. However, if you want to scale your company, you need to start creating a hierarchal structure with more specialized positions.

THE GROWTH PHASE, PART I: PREPARE FOR GROWTH

As companies begin to grow, you have to set up the organizational structure so the business runs more efficiently—and without you. To create a successful business structure, start with reading your mission statement, your *Why*. Then begin creating a process or workflow on how to best achieve your mission statement. While your mission statement is your *Why—why are we doing what we are doing each day*, your process is the *How—how do we get the job done*. From there, you will be ready to create a business structure.

You may ask, "Why start with a process chart to build an organizational chart?" The reason you start with a process is so that every part of your process has an "owner," someone responsible for making sure that process is run properly. This will ensure there are no gaps in responsibility, and when something goes wrong, you can easily identify who is in charge of fixing the problem.

Our mission statement is "To create loyal fans one move at a time." Our end game is to have unparalleled customer service so that our customers become fans. By creating fans, we generate more repeat and referral business and build a stellar reputation in the communities we serve.

Workflow

Draw out a workflow that follows a product or service through its life cycle. It can be elaborate or simple, but it should look somewhat like a timeline, starting with marketing or whatever you do to drive sales and ending with receiving payment by accounting or whatever happens after a product or service is sold. Some people might have a customer service follow-up process post-sale. Make sure you draw out every part of what needs to be done to complete the life cycle of your product or service.

After you draw out your workflow chart, start writing the job titles for who oversees each process. Next, start writing names of the people on your team next to the job titles they fit. You may find during this exercise that you have a gap in accountability, processes that don't have owners, and may need to hire someone to oversee a process. Notate the gap and make plans to hire someone to take charge of that part of the process. These will be strategic hires you will need to make in the future; however, until you hire that person, you need to temporarily put someone in charge so that there is a clearly defined person in charge of each part of the process.

THE GROWTH PHASE, PART II: SPIN OFF

In the Spin Off Phase, you will start adding more leaders and the company will become more delineated and specialized. As we grew, we added a Sales manager, or Sales leader, and created a Sales department. Although it might seem like overkill to have a manager for a small group (two people!), it is important for future scalability. Your company needs to grow into the structure, instead of out of it.

As your company grows, the number of people and processes within a department will outgrow a manager.

Too many people: If your manager has too many people to oversee and they are not able to mentor and train everyone on their team, you will need to add another manager or an assistant manager. The hierarchy of your company begins to have layers of management.

Too many processes: If the manger is stretched out from overseeing too many processes to run them efficiently, you will need to spin off part of the process and create a new department. This new department will have a new manager to lead it, and the new department will become more specialized.

The managers' work should be challenging; however, if they are overwhelmed because the department has grown too big for them, then your management team will suffer burnout, and that can cause a breakdown in the process, which will affect your overall efficiency.

Smaller companies frequently combine the Sales and Marketing departments. If you are doing this now, that is okay, but as soon as you are big enough, you need to start separating the two and treat them as different entities in your company. Marketing gets people interested in your brand, and sales takes interested people and turns them into customers. They are quite different, but in a start-up whose resources are limited, people often wear many hats.

For example, if you previously had Sales and Marketing grouped together and you spun off Marketing, you could hire someone with just marketing experience and no sales experience. Five years later, if your Marketing department starts becoming too big again, you might want to spin off digital marketing and hire a head of Digital Marketing. Again, you will have increased the level of specialization in your departments.

In small companies, one person often will run several processes. As I mentioned before, a person in charge of Sales might also be the Marketing head. It is also common for a receptionist to be the office manager and a bookkeeper to manage payroll and human resources. A person can be in charge of multiple processes, but make sure that two people are *not* in charge of the same process (this is discussed further in chapter twelve). This prevents a *responsibility dilution* in which no one wants to claim accountability for a task that goes wrong.

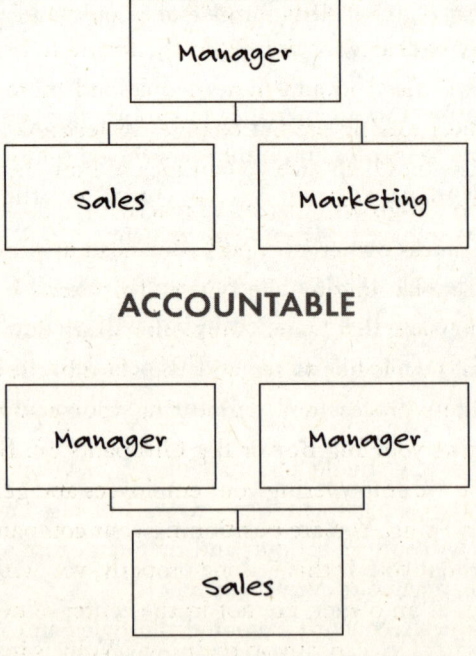

ACCOUNTABLE

ACCOUNTABILITY DILUTION

The goal for the spin-off stage is to develop highly specialized teams that are experts in what they do while you are growing your business. This happens gradually as profits grow and you have the ability to pay higher skilled employees who can fill the need of specialization.

THE MATURITY PHASE

As my company reached maturity, the teams became even more specialized. Now a manager is focused only on drivers, and customer service becomes its own department.

In this phase, the owner has moved out of the day-to-day business processes so that they are able to work on long-term strategic goals. I still look at my business as a 24/7 job, because when I am needed, I need to be there, but in the Maturity Phase, I have the resources to go on an extended vacation and enjoy more of my free time uninterrupted. When people are envious of an entrepreneur's lifestyle, they are envious of business owners in the Maturity Phase. Remember, it doesn't start off that way, and some businesses never get there because they get stuck in the Start-Up Phase and never build the infrastructure needed to scale to a mature business.

You can draw these charts for years into the future to brainstorm and figure out where you will need to add more people and more departments. Be flexible—you can never exactly predict changes in technology or the market. That said, the exercise does help give you an idea of how things might change so you can be proactive to growth instead of reactive.

Your job as a business owner is to pull your head up from the day-to-day activities and focus on planning for the future. This exercise is more of an art than a science. Make sure that, after completing your flowcharts, you share them with your team. People like to see how they fit into the big picture.

Creating a business process and delineating your company into departments is part of putting your Big Boy or Big Girl pants on. By setting up your company to scale, you are empowering your employees and getting yourself out of the middle of everything. You are positioning your company to scale up and someday operate without you. If this is done properly, you will have set up your company so that you, as an owner, are not in the center of everything and the people and processes in place can run on their own. Why is it so important that a company can run without you?

THE GROWTH PARADOX

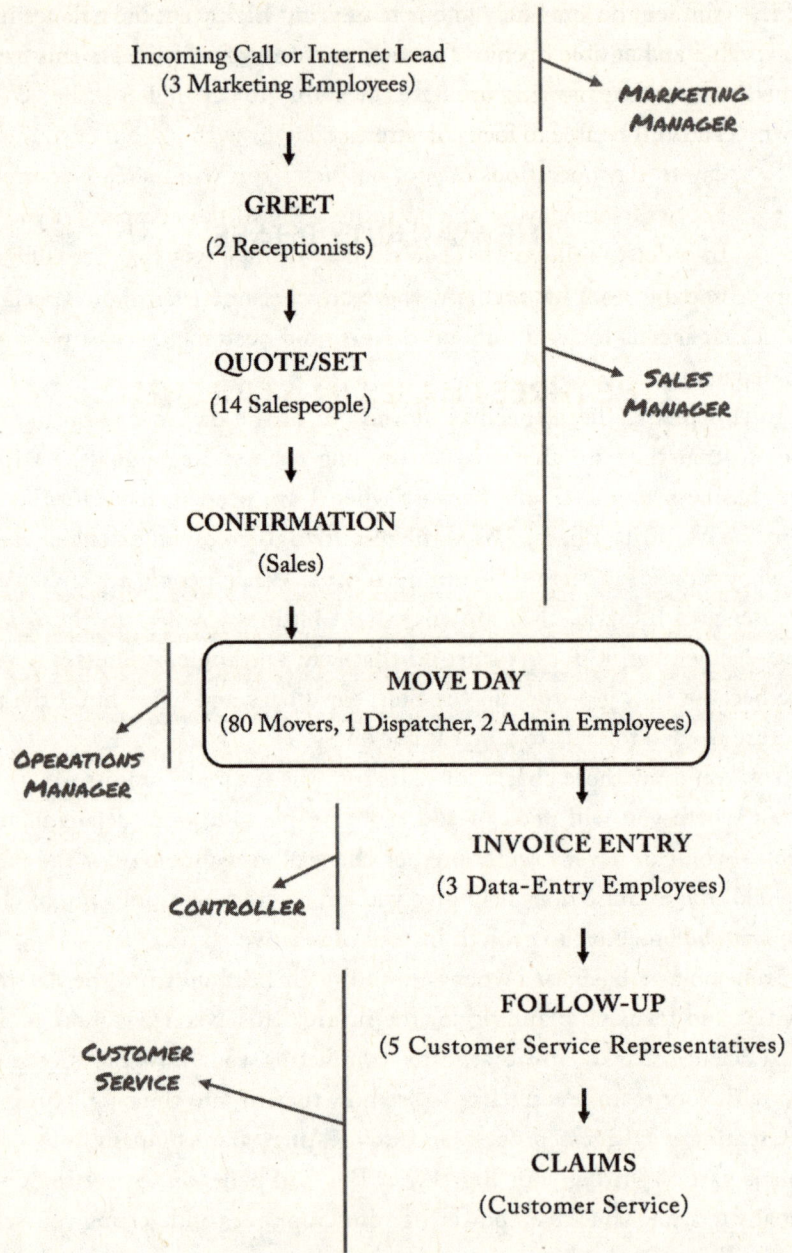

THE MATURITY PHASE:

5 Departments (Sales, Marketing, Operations, Accounting, Customer Service). 5 Managers, 30 Office Employees, 80 Movers.

- You will be less likely to burn out. You will have more balance in your life and be able to enjoy free time with your family and friends without your phone blowing up.
- You will be able to focus on strategy and growth instead of running the day-to-day operations of your business. This will increase your profits.
- You will someday be able to retire and sell the company if you wish. In order to sell, you have to show a future buyer that the company is valuable even without you at the helm.

THE THREE PHASES IN A NUTSHELL

THE START-UP PHASE

Characterized by the Chief-and-Many-Helpers model. The owner has all the control, and every decision goes through him or her. People gravitate to what they do best, but there is a lot of overlap in responsibilities. Often one person will wear many hats. For example, a sales manager might have that title, but might also oversee new business development, marketing, and customer service. An accountant might also manage all the human resource policies. The company is small enough so that everyone knows what each other is doing and can often roll up their sleeves to help each other when needed.

THE GROWTH PHASE

Part 1: Prepare for Growth

The beginning of specialization and the beginning of the decentralization of power. Departments start to form, and leaders are created who have authority other than the owner. The owner still might oversee a process, but his or her role in the day-to-day operations begins to decrease. Growing pains will occur in your departments, and you will have to spin off new departments.

In this phase, not every decision goes through the owner. There is still overlap between departments, so one person might be doing jobs from different parts of the process, but there is a definite division of work and more specialization than the Start-Up phase. Communication will need to be addressed as the company starts to grow. The team used to be one big team, and now as departments start to form, it is important to address cultural issues that may develop. The us-versus-them between departments can occur if you are not careful.

Part 2: Spin Off

Your company's hierarchy develops layers of management as the number of people and processes increase. You should monitor your managers' workloads: Their work should be challenging but not overwhelming, and if it is the latter, you should add another manager or assistant manager to avoid employee burnout.

You will need to spin off parts of processes to create new departments, which in turn will become more specialized. You now can hire people who are more specialized in their skills and experience. For example, instead of a marketing generalist, you may hire someone with digital marketing experience.

THE MATURITY PHASE

Power is completely decentralized. Managers are empowered to operate autonomously. Departments are highly specialized so that the owner will most likely not be able to roll up his or her sleeves and help. There is very little overlap between departments. Spin-offs are rarer and usually happen in response to market or product line changes. Communication is instrumental to ensure all departments are working harmoniously. Culture is a primary focus to keep the company from becoming fragmented.

END OF CHAPTER CHECKLIST

- ❏ I created a workflow chart, from start to finish with my product or service.
- ❏ I labeled the chart with the job titles of those who are responsible for each part of the process.
- ❏ I filled in the names of people who fit the job titles and identified accountability gaps.
- ❏ I have created a plan to fix the accountability gaps.
- ❏ No process has two managers in charge of it, but one manager may be in charge of two processes.

8

Don't Be That Asshole

Years ago, I was listening to a business friend vent about his company. He was completely at his wit's end—overworked and stressed. He didn't see a way out, and his team was upset with him because they were feeling unsupported. We were brainstorming what to do, and it seemed to both of us that he was doing too much, but it felt like nothing was getting done. As he discussed all his issues, it seemed that these were precisely all *his* issues: Every issue seemed to rest squarely on his shoulders alone. He was stressed about sales, accounting, and operations.

I asked him who were his direct reports. We then took out some paper and drew what appeared to be a functional organizational chart (see page 71).

As the conversation continued, he related issues he was having with people who were not his direct reports. For example, he had to talk with a salesperson about his lack of contacts put into the company's Customer Relationship Manager (CRM). He was missing inventory and had issues with his inventory control person. He was putting out fires in all areas of his company.

I asked him why people two levels away in his hierarchy chart were asking him questions instead of going to their direct manager. "Shouldn't your salesperson be speaking with your Sales manager?" I asked him to draw a line to

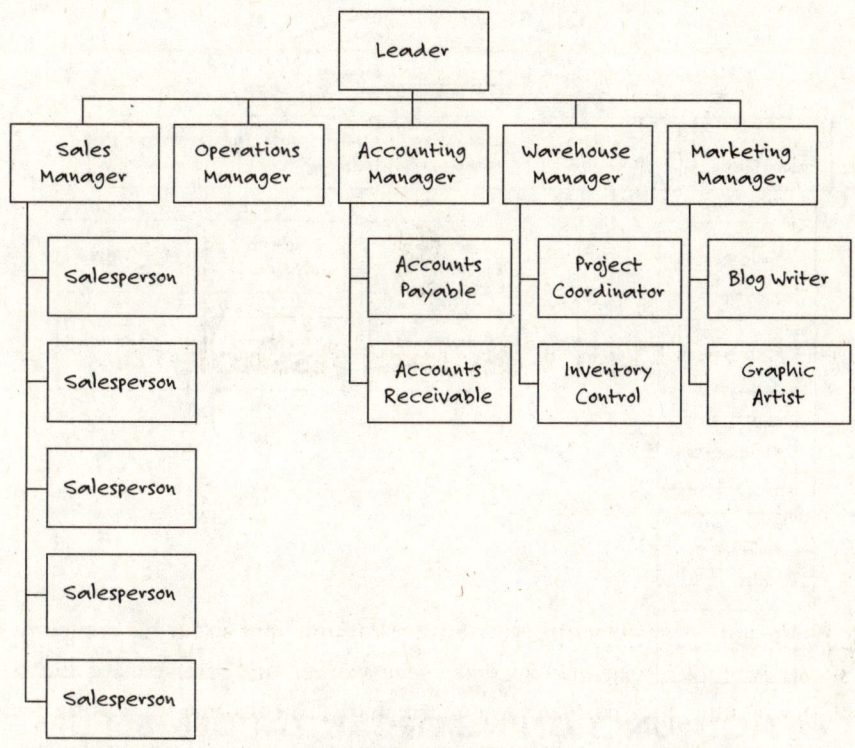

A HEALTHY ORGANIZATIONAL STRUCTURE

show me who else reports to him "from time to time." He updated the chart and showed me how for "certain things" and during "certain situations" people bypassed their manager and went to him directly. As he explained this, he started adding lines to his chart, and, in a matter of minutes, his organizational chart started looking like football plays (see page 72, top).

I redrew the chart so that it reflected the way his company actually functioned (see page 72, bottom).

He looked at the new chart, agreeing that it captured the situation precisely. People were coming at him from all directions with issues. Just looking at the chart made him feel anxious.

By then we had had a few drinks, which probably contributed to my snarky remark. I pointed out that the chart I drew looked like a giant asshole. We began to laugh. Every decision, every task, every question went through him.

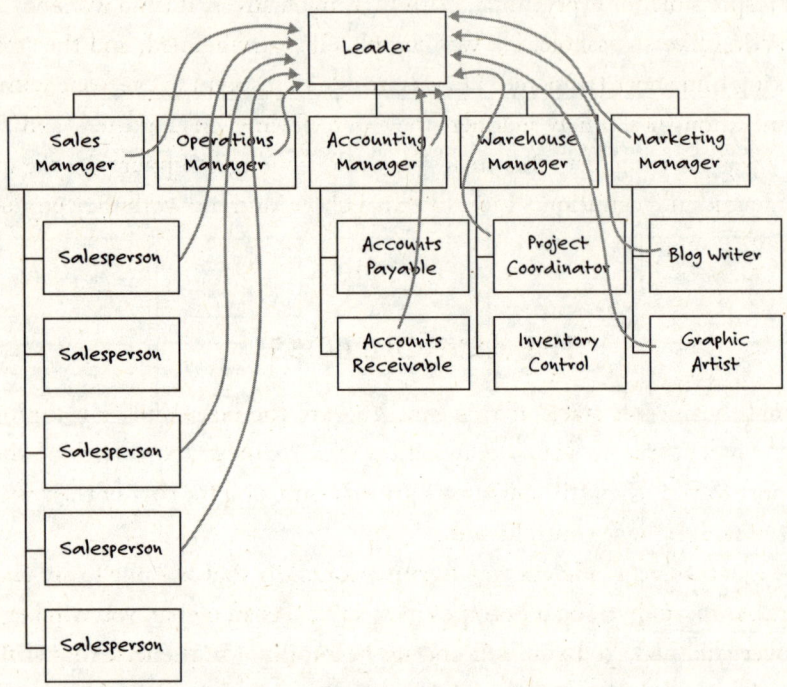

A NONFUNCTIONING ORGANIZATION—SET UP CORRECTLY BUT OPERATES INCORRECTLY

WHAT A NONFUNCTIONING ORGANIZATION FEELS LIKE

He was responsible for everything. With that much stress, it is no wonder that he was acting like an asshole. He was completely overwhelmed, and the stress was making him short-tempered. He was unable to respond to everyone within his organization in a timely manner, they were feeling unsupported, and the company was growing fast—his structure could no longer support the organization. He said in frustration, "I feel like an asshole, and the work they produce now is shit."

"THE ASSHOLE BOSS"

Most small businesses start off this way. You are the boss, and as you grow, you add more people to your organization who report to you. Even if they don't report to you, they still must get sign-offs from you for part of their work because you might have control issues.

This is actually an efficient way to run a company that has one to six team members. At more than six, it becomes ineffective. As an owner, you will begin to feel overwhelmed, and you will end up becoming a bottleneck that stifles your team's growth because you won't have the bandwidth to respond to everyone's needs in a timely and efficient manner. There are finite hours in each day, and you won't be able to be involved in every decision if you want your company to grow. Your team will get frustrated, you will get snippy, and, *presto*, you will be labeled as "that asshole."

We all have heard people say that their bosses are assholes. Usually, we feel sorry for the employee. Understanding it from the business owner's perspective, I feel sorry for the asshole owner too. He probably doesn't want to be an asshole, but with all the stress coming at him from every direction, he is overwhelmed. So how do you prevent yourself from being that asshole?

There are two reasons that the asshole structure occurs:

1. You set up the organizational structure incorrectly in the first place, like a giant rake, with you at the top and everyone reporting to you so that there is no hierarchy (see page 74). Such an owner often displays trust and control issues and is unable to delegate. Unless you abandon this belief system, you will be unable to grow your company.
2. Or, more often, you set up the right structure (as my business friend did), but you operate your company in a way that doesn't align with

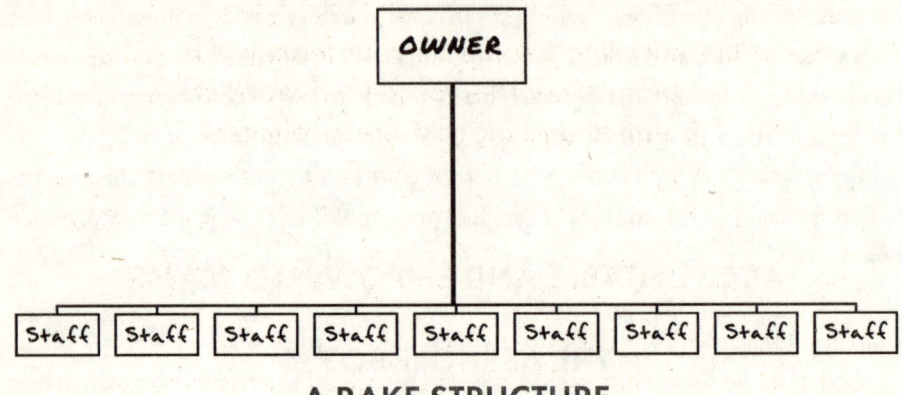

A RAKE STRUCTURE

the structure you set up, like the football play chart. You feel the need to get involved at every level because you either are afraid someone on your team will make a mistake, or simply you believe that you can do it better. Granted, you might actually be able to do certain jobs better; however, you need to get comfortable with a margin of error if you want to grow your business.

In an asshole structure, with you at the center of every decision, every problem comes at you from all directions. This approach to leadership has its advantages. You get to be the superhero. You get to solve everyone's problems, and you get to feel needed.

If you are running a small company, this allows you to be in total control of everything. Maybe you like it that way because you are a bit of a control freak and want to sign off on everything. Or maybe you like the feeling of being needed and you like being the "go-to" person.

Alternatively, you may have set up the organization correctly with a hierarchy and layers of management, but nevertheless you operate like an asshole. Basically, you undermine your managers so that their direct reports have to go around them and come directly to you in order to function within your organization. Or you don't empower your managers to make decisions on their own.

Empowering people on your team will be the biggest contributor to your work-life balance and will be your biggest stress reliever. I repeat:

> *Empowering people on your team will be the biggest contributor to your work-life balance and biggest stress reliever.*

ACCOUNTABLE AND EMPOWERED TEAMS

I am friends with lots of business owners, and the ones with *accountable* teams rarely get phone calls while we are at lunch or attending a meeting because their teams are empowered to make decisions. These business owners are usually the ones with the largest companies. Coincidence? Not at all: The "big guys" have the structure in place to scale their company properly. The ones who are struggling with accountability are the ones whose cell phones are ringing off the hook. Not only is their work-life balance affected, but they are prevented from working strategically on their business because they are too busy putting out daily fires.

You have probably heard the expression to work *on* your business and not *in* your business. An empowered workforce will allow you to do just that. If you are not busy in the day-to-day operations, you can focus on strategic growth initiatives.

At this point in creating your foundation for growth, you have a customer-focused mission statement and a process diagram with each part of the process labeled, including job titles and names. Now you are ready to draw up an organizational chart ensuring that managers oversee certain people and processes within your company.

Next, you need to delegate authority within your organization. Empower your people so they can operate without you being at the center of every decision. You can do this by completing two exercises: 1) create bullet job descriptions, and 2) give your direct reports authority to make decisions without you. Both exercises should be documented and shared with your team.

Setting up formal processes, job descriptions, decision authorities, and other activities outlined in this book will help when you have employee turnover. It is much easier to hand a new hire a bullet-form job description, vision statement, process flow, and other written aspects of their job than to tell them to shadow someone and hope they absorb their job through on-the-job training, which is just what my company used to do, unsuccessfully. If you don't have your processes written down, they will break down when you experience worker turnover.

Bullet Job Descriptions

From your Process Diagram, take the title of each role and make a list of everything they are in charge of doing. I would engage the person who is in this position to help with the list. You might see some hesitation here because when you ask people what they do every day, they sometimes become defensive, worried about proving their value to the company.

Explain to your teammates that you are drawing out responsiblities for each position and you need to understand who is accountable for what so that there is more clarity about responsibility throughout the company. Most likely they are doing something that you are not even aware they are doing. You might also notice some redundancy if they are performing tasks that they shouldn't be performing and that should fall under someone else's purview. In the end, it should look like a mini job description in bullet form.

The sample job descriptions on page 77 are from my industry. Yours will look different.

Decision Authority

After you create accountability bullet points, you need to go one step further with accountability. From a speaker named Eric Coryell, an expert in accountability, I learned that to create efficiency within your company, you should make a list of all the major decisions a person in a role would need to own.

Classify the authority level needed for each decision by using the following categories:

LEVEL 1: Owner's Decision
LEVEL 2: Manager's Decision (*Discuss with Owner First*)
LEVEL 3: Manager's Decision (*Tell Owner Later*)
LEVEL 4: Manager's Decision (*Owner Doesn't Need to Know*)

OWNER

Vision

Problem-Solving

Big Relationships

Long-term Growth Strategies

Mentoring Department Heads

Real Estate

Taxes/Legal

OPERATIONS MANAGER

Customer Service/Claims

Facilities

Crew Leaders

Vendor Relations

Dispatch

Capacity

Regulations

Compliance Safety

SALES

Sales Strategy

Goals & Revenue

Sales Process

Inbound/Outbound

Lead/Opportunity Nurturing

People Development and Management

MARKETING

SEO and Online Lead Generation

Website

Customer Experience

Social Media/Online Reputation

Brand Awareness & Guidelines

Community Outreach

CONTROLLER

A/R & A/P

Inventory Control

Payroll/401k & 529

Tax Filings

Budget/Forecast

Financial Reporting

Insurance Renewal and Maintenance

Related Companies

DIRECTOR OF TECHNOLOGY

Software & Hardware

Network Security

Systems Architecture

Information Systems Management

IT Vendor Contracts

Disaster Recovery

Website Functionality

Technology Budget

DECISION AUTHORITY

DECISION	LEVEL	DECISION-MAKER
Raises over budget	1	Owner
Raises under budget	3	Manager (Tell owner later)
Termination	2	Manager (Discuss with owner first)
New core software	1	Owner
Customer refund under $1,000	4	Manager (Owner doesn't need to know)
Customer refund over $1,000	3	Manager (Tell owner later)
Promotions	2	Manager (Discuss with owner first)
Accidents/Claims	1	Owner
Schedule changes	4	Manager (Owner doesn't need to know)
PTO requests up to a few days	4	Manager (Owner doesn't need to know)
PTO requests longer than 1 week	3	Manager (Tell owner later)
New hire/Outside plan	1	Owner
New hire/Inside plan	4	Manager (Owner doesn't need to know)
HR policy change	1	Owner
Banking change	1	Owner
Benefits change	1	Owner
Regular inventory purchase	4	Manager (Owner doesn't need to know)
Purchase outside of norm	2	Manager (Discuss with owner first)

You have built a Decision Authority chart that helps clarify authority.

Level 1: Owner's Decision

"Owner's Decisions" are decisions that must go through the business owner and are theirs alone to make. The bigger you grow and the more formalized processes you have in place, the fewer decisions there will be for the owner to make.

Owner's Decisions might include all decisions about wages, hiring, and firing. Obviously, the CEO of an airline company is not going to know if Gary in the baggage department at the Atlanta airport was terminated because he was late. However, Sally, the head of a small café, might want to know if her day manager was going to fire the hostess. A small company whose business owner is carefully managing its cash-flow would want to give approval for all raises. A larger company would manage these decisions with set processes. For example, we budget a certain percentage of our payroll each year so that managers can give their teams raises. This is how we utilize processes to allow managers to act without the owner's input. If managers want to go above the budgeted allocation for raises, they need to have the owner's permission first, which is a Level 1 Decision.

Level 2: Manager's Decision (Discuss with Owner First)

My managers can fire anyone in their departments without my permission. We go over this decision as a group first to make sure we are all in alignment, but ultimately the manager will have full authority over who stays on his or her team.

I believe that managers should have full authority to hire and fire their direct reports. I like to know ahead of time so I can counsel them to consider other options, if necessary, but ultimately it is their decision. As an owner, if you plan to hold your manager accountable for their departmental goals, they have to be able to pick the people on their team. It would be unfair for me to hold my manager and her department accountable for hitting their goals if she lacks confidence in her team's performance.

Level 3: Manager's Decision (Tell Owner Later)

This is for decisions such as giving a team member a week off for vacation. I like to know where people are, but I don't need to be involved in the decision to approve their PTO. A simple email that "Arnie is going on vacation the last week of December" is good enough to keep me in the loop. Performance reviews, raises within budget, termination of non-key employees, and switching vendors are all decisions that my managers can make on their own; however, this wasn't always the case.

Level 4: Manager's Decision (Owner Doesn't Need to Know)

This is for all small decisions that are normal parts of the company's daily process that your team should be able to make on their own without your input. Examples of these decisions may be refunds to customers, documenting an employee's file for poor performance, or negotiating better terms with a vendor.

As your company grows, you will let go of your authority and give more power to your management team. Small business owners want to know everything that is going on, while large business owners are focused on strategy and not the day-to-day details. This is understandable if you equate the cost of failure to the total annual revenue. A $10,000 decision in a million-dollar company carries more weight than in a billion-dollar company. Your business will stay small if you have to sign off on every decision because eventually you will become a bottleneck that will slow down your company's growth.

END OF CHAPTER CHECKLIST

Ask yourself the following questions to determine if you are preventing your company from scaling.

- ❏ Am I currently at the center of all decisions, even ones that could be solved with a written process?
- ❏ What does my current organizational chart look like?
- ❏ Does the chart work as drawn or am I undermining my management team by allowing their direct reports to come to me for issues?

- ❏ Have I created bullet point descriptions for each job title within my company and reviewed them with my employees to ensure accuracy?
- ❏ Have I made a list of all decisions that need to be made on a daily basis to run my company and assigned a Decision Authority Level to each one?
- ❏ Have I shared this chart with my management team?

9

Don't Rely Solely on Financials

I had been running a business for several years when I decided I wanted to go back to college and finish my degree. When I dropped out of my undergraduate studies, I was less than a year away from getting my BA in art, but after my father had a stroke, I never returned. I realized that I didn't need an art degree—instead, I needed an education in business.

When I started back at 3 Men Movers, I knew nothing about running a business and could not read a basic financial statement. This was in the early 2000s, before the Internet—I had to go to the city library to find books on business and accounting. I had to teach myself the meaning of cost of goods, fixed and variable expenses, gross revenue, and net profits. I was lost when it came to business basics, and so I went back to school and got my MBA from Rice University in Houston.

At Rice, I received a phenomenal business education; however, there were a few things that I thought were missing, particularly the importance of *key indicators*. Key indicators are also referred to as Key Performance Indicators, or KPIs. These are business metrics, which are not necessarily financial metrics, that measure the performance of various aspects of your company. We were taught accounting, finance, and economics. We learned how to read financial sheets and analyze data. What we didn't learn was how to create and monitor key business indicators. Luckily, my Vistage 812 group had a guest speaker, Kraig Kramers, now deceased, who taught us the importance of metrics, which I'm sharing with you.

SAVE THE MONTH

While timely and accurate financials are important and should be reviewed monthly, they are limited in their ability to help you steer your company's ship. Normally, you receive your income statement and balance sheet sometime during the second week of the month for the previous month. If you are lucky, you may get it sooner, but Accounting still needs to reconcile everything before you get to review the financial reports.

Let's say you get your income statement (profit and loss) by May 12 for the month of April. You review it and notice that the profits aren't what you want them to be. You start to dig. Did you overspend? You compare April to March's expenses and then year over year, and the expenses seem like they're in line with the previous month. Nothing seems out of order.

You have to keep digging. Is it sales? You look at your revenue and notice that it does look lower year over year, but that only gives you part of the picture. From your income statement, there is no way of discerning if it is a sales performance issue or a marketing issue. Incoming leads are not included in an income statement, so you have to ask Marketing. Marketing blames Sales and their closing rates, but Sales says that the leads are down. As you keep digging to find out what the problem is, you are losing precious time that could be used for fixing the problem.

You finally figure out that one of your salespeople is not closing leads, but by then you have lost precious time. It is now closer to the end of May. You quickly create a plan of action to correct the situation. You are now at the end of the month, so you institute these changes ASAP, hoping that you will see some results during June. May is already gone, and you completely lost the opportunity to change that month. The problem is you will still have to wait for financial reports to be released in the middle of July to see if the plan you created fixed the issue in June.

You work all through June to correct the issue. Mid-July comes along, and you look once more at your financial reports. You still are unhappy with the results. Again, you have to dig, and by the time the plan is in place, you have wasted all of July.

You are always two steps behind if you are making decisions based on mid-month financial reports. You are always looking backward, never able to take a proactive approach so that you can change your course of action quickly enough to affect your current month.

Financials are great for looking back, but they are horrible for helping you run your company better. When you run a business, you need to be able to make decisions quickly based on real-time data, not historical monthly reports. You need numbers fast. Some numbers you need to look at daily and some weekly. Getting these numbers quickly will help you be proactive in your response to changes within your company. You might even be able to save the month by identifying problems and putting actions in place at the beginning of the month instead of two weeks into the following month.

KEY INDICATORS ARE KEY

If it were up to me, there would be a whole class in all MBA programs dedicated exclusively to KPIs. Key indicators are the most valuable tool you will use to decide when and how to tweak your business activities to keep on course toward your goals.

For example, the KPIs we monitor in our Marketing department are leads, and we check them daily, weekly, and monthly. Let's take the same situation from above, but instead of reviewing financials monthly, we catch the exact issue immediately with weekly key indicators. We had a key indicator for each salesperson's performance and we noticed that one of our salespersons was burning through our leads. We can immediately solve and test our solution each week and ultimately save the month.

Income statements help you run your business like a large ship. If you are cruising along and find out too late that you've taken a wrong turn, it takes a long time to slow down and maneuver the ship. Key indicators allow you to operate like a small speed boat. With these numbers, you can zig and zag and change direction fast.

You should have simple reports for the company's overall performance, each department's performance, and individual team members' performance. A daily key indicator that we monitor is *service levels* (which is an indication of how long on average our customers on the phone are placed on hold), and if the levels are low, meaning customers are spending a long time on hold, it could mean we are short-staffed. We figured out what went wrong and put a plan in place to fix it immediately. Effective businesses track several key indicators. We look at incoming lead count, closing ratios by agent, numbers of different services sold, and so on. These are examples of what we monitor, but your business will be different based on your industry.

If a salesperson is suddenly performing poorly in April, you should find out in a weekly meeting in April and not on May 12 when you receive your income statement and notice your profits aren't where they are supposed to be. If you find out quickly, you can take action and reverse the issue quickly, which will hopefully save your month.

Key indicators aren't a secret scoring system for the owner and the managers to use to evaluate performance. Everyone within your company should know which key indicator they are graded on. They should also know their department's key indicators and the company's big key indicators. Not every business owner feels comfortable sharing their financials with their team, but your team wants to know how the business is doing.

> **Showing up for work every day and not knowing how the company is performing is like playing a game and never knowing the score.**

Key indicators are a great way to share how the company is doing as a whole. You can share the number of jobs completed year-to-date versus last year and the percentage of increase or decrease. You can share the department's on-time score. And while there are thousands of things you can track, just because you can track something doesn't mean you should. You must be careful not to track too many numbers, only ones that lead to corrective actions to improve your business.

> *Remember, when everything is important, nothing is important.*

CREATING KEY INDICATORS

Start with the accountability chart you previously drew out and look at the bullet tasks next to each name. Now ask yourself the following: *If I could find out with three or fewer numbers how an employee is performing, which three numbers would they be, and how often would I need to check them?*

Start writing the types of key indicators you would like to track. Make sure the numbers are relatively easy to gather, as you don't want to create more work for your team (if your team is digging through data trying to create key indicator reports, they might spend too much time on reporting and lose track of their mission). Then review your process chart and think about what makes your company successful. Think about each department and what each department is responsible for to ensure your company is successful and add key indicators to track your progress.

Here are some key indicator ideas:

SERVICE COMPANY	MARKETING
On-Time Score	# of Leads
Net Promoter Score (NPS)	# of Requests for Demos
Site Inspections	# of Incoming Phone Calls
Inspections	
Damages/Complaints	

Leading Key Indicators

External leading indicators are indicators in the economy used to predict how your business will perform in the future. A straightforward example to imagine a company's use of external leading key indicators is an umbrella company tracking the weather. If there has been a drought that's lasted several years, this would affect sales. If a rainy season is predicted, the umbrella company would start producing more umbrellas to prepare for an increase in umbrella sales. In this example, the weather forecast would be their leading key indicator. Leading indicators are like crystal-ball key indicators. Leading key indicators foretell your future revenue projections. For example, if new home starts are down, home sales will be down and, as a result, moving services will be down as well. Other companies affected by new home starts might be window blinds, mortgage companies, residential carpet companies, and home appliance stores. You will want to track leading indicators so that you can prepare for an increase or a decrease in business. Do you need to hire more people and put in more resources to prepare for a burst of business, or freeze everything to prepare for a recession?

There are internal leading indicators that will help you project business volume too. For example, if you are monitoring your sales pipeline or incoming marketing opportunities and notice a dip, it will probably result in a dip in your income in the future if you don't take immediate corrective action. As you get familiar with your numbers, you will know from your sales cycle exactly when the dip in marketing opportunities will affect the revenue of your company. Being successful is about more than just financial success—therefore, you should be tracking other metrics like customer reviews, on-time scores, and safety metrics. If safety is important at your company, you can also track incidents that might lead to future accidents. For example, the GPS systems on our trucks track unsafe driving. This data can be used as a predictor of an increased number of accidents. You need to monitor these indicators daily and weekly to understand the connection before they can become effective as key indicators.

When you set up your key indicators, make sure you do so in a way that everyone on your team can easily understand. There are some special people who love spreadsheets, and then there are most people, like me, who need cartoon-like, colorful graphs. The use of colors and graphs help because they will resonate with most people (unless you are running an engineering firm; engineers love big spreadsheets).

If your business is seasonal, compare year-over-year numbers—for example, looking at this March compared to March last year. If your business isn't seasonal, you can compare this week with last week or this month with last month. If the number you are tracking is below what it should be, make sure it shows up in red. If it is going in the right direction, show the number in green. Now, your team can easily see the key indicators that track their individual performance as part of their department as well as the company as whole, and can see how it is progressing over time.

Numbers can be overwhelming for some people, so keep that in mind. Keep it simple so the people on your team are not turned off by being inundated with numbers. Make sure you get feedback on how the key indicators are presented so you can ensure that your team fully understands them. Decide also how often to track your key indicators: daily, weekly, monthly, quarterly, or yearly. Each manager should be in charge of their department's key indicators as well as each individual's key indicators within the department.

TWEAKING *KEY* KEY INDICATORS

As you begin tracking these numbers, you will find that some are not important. Maybe they rarely change, and they don't seem to help you gauge your business. If that is the case, then stop tracking those numbers and replace them with numbers that are important. Remember, this is a work in progress.

Sometimes you will have an issue with a product line or a new project or process that is important to track. You can add a temporary key indicator to track that issue daily until you have it worked out. These are like training wheels; once the issue has corrected itself and everything is running smoothly, you can stop tracking those key indicators.

The economy is cyclical. Businesses normally ebb and flow along with the economy, and you will find yourself in a constant struggle to outsmart the economy's cycles. Sometimes you won't be so lucky, and your business will suffer. Remember that during these times you are still the same person you were when things were going well. Don't attach your emotional well-being to the roller coaster of a normal economic business cycle.

Don't let your income statement and balance sheet define you.

END OF CHAPTER CHECKLIST

- ❑ I have identified KPIs for each position, department, and for the overall well-being of the company.
- ❑ I have considered what drives my business both internally and externally and defined some leading key indicators.
- ❑ I have created a written process for pulling the data to create key indicators and have delegated the process.
- ❑ I have presented these key indicators in a way my employees can easily understand, using colors and graphs.
- ❑ I have asked for feedback from my team on the key indicators to ensure that they are relevant and helpful.
- ❑ I have scheduled time during daily, weekly, and monthly meetings to review the key indicators with my team and share their individual and departmental progress with them.

10
Running Fat and Skinny

If you are going to build a skyscraper, you need to either start on bedrock or start digging and pouring concrete beams with steel rebar. The same is true if you want to build a large company. People who marvel at skyscrapers look up, but often discount what is below the surface. Similarly, people who want to build a large company focus on sales revenue and discount the importance of creating a solid foundation. The taller the building, the stronger the foundation needs to be, and the same is true for a company.

Creating a foundation for a company consists of a litany of tasks. It starts with having a purposeful mission statement, documented processes, accountable people, scalable software, and a strong leadership team. Creating your foundation costs money, so you must be careful not to burn up your cash.

Remember:

Revenue is Vanity.
Profits are Sanity.
Cash is King.

And then there is the most important rule of business:

Don't run out of cash!

While this seems logical, 70 percent of businesses fail before their tenth year.* Most business owners focus on generating top-line gross sales revenue to ensure their cash positions. When you hear business owners bragging that they made millions in revenue, that doesn't tell you much. It isn't how much you make that matters; it is how much you keep after expenses. Consider two companies, one with revenue of three million a year and another pulling in only one million in annual revenue. At first glance, you would think the first company is the more successful one; however, if the net margin is 5 percent because the company can't control its costs, then its net earnings are only $150,000 a year. The second company, on the other hand, has a healthy net profit margin of 18 percent and therefore is bringing in $180,000 a year. This is a good example of why you shouldn't be impressed with revenue numbers.

In the second year I owned 3 Men Movers, I was focused on the amount of top-line revenue we were going to make, and everything was pointing to us having an amazing year. We were growing fast, and I needed to hire people and invest in technology to keep up with the growth.

Having little business experience, I lost sight of my expenses and was surprised to find out, unfortunately, at the end of the year, that although we made more gross revenue, our expenses outpaced our revenue, and year over year we made less in profits. We worked harder but made less money! This was an amateur mistake, but an easy one to make. If I am not cautious, it is a mistake that can easily be repeated even today.

Rapid growth can kill a company as easily as lack of sales, but it is more of a silent killer. Rapid growth makes you feel like you are successful, and while you are focused on the money rolling in the front door, you can easily lose sight of the additional expenses needed to support the increase in sales that is pouring out the back door. Low sales creates panic, and the panic leads you to be more

---

* For more information, see https://www.fundera.com/blog/what-percentage-of-small-businesses-fail.

mindful of your costs. Rapid growth distracts you with the feeling of success, and while you are managing an increase in business, it is busy destroying your profit margin because you are spending to keep up with growth. Don't let this silent killer sneak up on you.

There are three ways to prevent rapid growth from eroding your profit margin:

1. Plan for growth.
2. Understand how growth affects your profits and monitor it. This means monitoring financials, especially expense ratio reports, and key indicators.
3. Don't solve problems by throwing money at them. (See #1. Again, plan for growth!)

GROWTH GOALS

If you start your company's growth journey without planning out the human resources you will need at various stages, you will be destined to hire in a panic because you'll need someone *right now*, which leads to bad hires, or you will end up firing employees who are unprepared for the company you will become. Without planning, your future company will leave behind good employees who haven't been prepared for growth. Project your human resource needs in advance so that you can plan and budget for new hires.

The people on your team are the single biggest component in determining your company's success. You can't win the World Series with a bunch of B-level and C-level players.

Look around at your current team and think about your growth goals. Are your people capable of running the company that you foresee in the future? Remember that a person who can run a sales team of a $500,000-a-year company might not be the person to run a sales team of a $5 million company, and the person who is running a $5 million company might not be able to make the jump to running a $50 million company.

If you have confidence in an employee's ability to adapt and grow with your company, but the employee doesn't have experience running larger teams, you will need to plan on getting him or her the training and mentorship necessary in order to grow with your organization. You should always be thinking about the company you will have five to ten years from now and what you will need to do today to make sure you have the human resources and structure for your future company.

Be cognizant of your current team members' abilities and how they will adjust to the increased demands of a larger business. Think about the job description you would have posted to hire someone to run a department of a company with $1 million in annual revenue and compare it to the job description you would place for the person who runs a department with $10 million in annual revenue—the description would be quite different. Your expectations and qualifications would be different too.

Your people will not magically acquire these skill sets while they are working for you. As a business owner, you have a responsibility to make sure you train your people to meet the increasing demands of their job. Your goal is to grow your current team's skills at the same speed at which you grow your company. This will require investment in training and mentoring. You might be worried about investing so much in an employee who might eventually leave, but that is a necessary risk you have to be willing to take.

> *"The only thing worse than training your employees and having them leave is not training them and having them stay."* —Henry Ford, Founder, Ford Motor Company

EVALUATE READINESS FOR GROWTH

What will your company look like if it doubles in size? Evaluate your company's foundation. Is it ready for growth? You have to look at the following:

1. **Leadership:** Evaluate your management team.
2. **Technology:** Determine if your CRM, accounting, marketing, and any industry-specific software is scalable.
3. **Processes:** What can be automated? Will your processes work efficiently with double or triple the amount of business?
4. **Quantity of People:** How many more people will you need?

5. **Quality of People:** Will your current people need training on new systems and strategies? Do they support the company's vision for the future?
6. **Organizational Structure:** Will you need to divide groups into more departments? Maybe it is time to separate Sales from Marketing. Maybe it is time to add a business development team.
7. **Facilities:** Do you have enough space to house the people and machinery needed when you scale? People often forget this one and commit to a ten-year lease when in ten years they project to have three times as many people. Where will these people sit? Where will you house your inventory?

BACKCASTING

If you want to grow your business, start by setting it up for growth. While forecasting is done by looking at trends and trying to predict what the future will bring, *backcasting* is the way to create an organized path that will get you to your business goals. To backcast, you look at what you need to have in place to reach your forecasted future.

When you are ready to grow your company, start off by completing a backcasting exercise. You will refer to this document as you grow to keep you on track with changes you need to implement to prepare for growth. This document is a working document and will change as you replace projections with real data. If you don't hit your revenue growth projections, you will need to retool and adjust your backcasting plan.

To start, lock yourself up somewhere so that you can focus on working on your business without distractions and create a Backcasting Chart. A sample chart is on page 95, but yours will look different depending on your size, industry, and growth projections. This exercise will help you plan for growth.

Backcasting Exercise

Step 1: Start by creating a small spreadsheet. Using Excel or Google Sheets will make this task easier, but if you are low-tech, you can use a piece of white paper, a ruler, and a pencil. It takes a lot more time, but in the end, you will arrive at the same place.

Projected Growth	20%	Current	Year 1	Year 2	Year 3	Year 4	Year 5+
Gross Revenue		$1,000,000	$1,200,000	$1,440,000	$1,728,000	$2,073,600	...
Cost of Goods	65%	$650,000	$780,000	$936,000	$1,123,200	$1,347,840	...
Gross Profit		$350,000	$420,000	$504,000	$604,800	$725,760	...
Operating Expenses	22%	$220,000	$264,000	$316,800	$380,160	$456,192	...
Net Profit	13%	$130,000	$156,000	$187,200	$224,640	$269,568	...
Business Needed							
Leads Needed		100	120	144	173	207	...
Services or Jobs Closing Rate 50%		50	60	72	86	104	...
Current Leaders							
Operations Manager: Robin		Yes	Replace				...
Marketing Manager: Kylie		Yes	Training SEO	Continuous	Continuous	Continuous	...
Accountant: Jennifer		Yes	Yes	Yes	Yes	Yes	
						Add controller	...
Sales Manager: Jim		Yes	Yes	Yes	Yes	Yes	...
Staffing By Department							
Sales Reps		5	6	7	9	10	...
Warehouse Staff		2	2.4	2.9	3.5	4.1	...
Accounting Staff		4	4.8	5.8	6.9	8.3	...
Number in Management Team		4	4	4	4	4	...
Total Head Count		15	17.2	19.8	23	26.8	...
Space Needed			Need larger office/warehouse space				
Software System			Upgrade to QuickBooks Pro				

Step 2: Create columns. Create columns with the future years going across the top. Your first column should be labeled "Current," and the next will be one year into the future until you have projected at least five years out.

Step 3: Create rows. Next, figure out a reasonable amount of growth you would like to achieve each year. Under cells with the years will be your current top-line revenue number for each year. Each year, you will increase that number by the percentage of growth that you hope to achieve. In the example chart on page 95, I projected a company that would grow by 15 percent each year.

Step 4: Forecast financials. Begin to fill in the rest of the rows with your important financial numbers listed down the side. It is up to you as to how many financial details to include. You won't need all the details, but you will want at least some of the big financial numbers. Here are some examples:

- **Gross Revenue** (the total amount of sales). You might want to break it down by product and goods offered or by geographic locations.
- **Cost of Goods (COGs)** (the direct cost attributable to the production of goods or services provided, which includes direct materials and labor costs). Note, this should increase when sales increase and decrease when sales decrease. It should always be a fixed ratio to the revenue line, varying little each month. If the ratio between your COGs and your gross revenue fluctuates each month, then you have a problem.
- **Operating Expenses.** Some of the items will be a percentage of the revenue number, like advertising, payroll, and office supplies. Other items will be relatively stable regardless of whether the revenue increases or decreases, like rent and utilities—that is, until you need a larger building. You may want to add a bit each year to account for inflation. This includes items like payroll, rent, and utilities. Regardless of what you sell, operating expenses will stay relatively the same.
- **Industry-Specific Data/Key Indicators.** Analyze the number of jobs or services that need to be sold to reach your projected goal.

Step 5: Keep adding metrics. Create more rows and move down the line, examining the resources needed to create growth. You know your industry. What will you need to grow? There is inflation, and you can certainly raise your prices each year for your services and products sold, but then you would also need to increase the cost to make these items and the cost of all your expenses. You can get very detailed, but I like to keep things simple and conservative, so I don't raise prices for the purpose of this exercise.

Step 6: Analyze human resources. There are two categories for analyzing human resources: quality and quantity.

Quality: Make a list of everyone on your leadership team and ask yourself if they can run a company with the revenue that you expect to hit five years from now. Jessica is doing a good job now, but will she be the right person five years from now? If not, can she be with the proper training? If she fits your culture, then you need to take steps to get her the training she needs to grow with the company. If you don't think Jessica has the capacity to grow with the company, even with training, then you need to make a plan to replace her with a better, more qualified candidate.

Quantity: Look at the head count per department. Do easy math and multiply the head count by the growth percentage. If you have ten people in sales and they are working at full capacity, in a year, at 20 percent growth, you will need twelve people, and if you double in your fifth year, you will need twenty sales agents. Again, do a gut check. Does this seem logical? Is there any way you can improve or automate your processes so that you can scale the company more efficiently and not have a 1-to-1 ratio of hiring more employees for your projected growth plans? Maybe your team is not running at full capacity, and instead of hiring another ten more sales agents when you double in sales, you could hire eight.

If you are going from one thousand jobs in a year to two thousand jobs five years from now, again, it becomes a mathematical equation. If everyone is currently operating at maximum efficiency, then in ten years if you don't improve your processes or automate any part, the head count of your entire company will need to double.

What will that mean for your company?

Step 7: Infrastructure and capital expenses. Is the office space you are in big enough? If you are in manufacturing, do you have enough storage for inventory and machinery to double in size? If not, think about how and when you should plan to move into a larger office space. Do you have the capital for a new warehouse if one is needed? Don't forget about the capital you might need to purchase new machines. If your manufacturing plant is building one hundred thousand widgets a year and that doubles, what sort of capital expenses will you need to invest in machinery to increase your output?

Step 8: Technology. Look at your software systems. Will your current systems be able to scale with your company's growth? If your systems are currently inefficient and sluggish, adding more volume will only make it worse. Can you possibly improve your software and automate certain jobs so that you don't have to hire as many people to keep up with growth?

This is a thinking exercise. Keep asking yourself questions that help you understand what resources are needed to support future growth, and what you will need in resources to hit your growth numbers. Look at how many leads you need to create sales. When doing this, try to get into the mindset of what your company will look and feel like five years from now. Do a gut check. Does this seem doable? If not, why? What do you need to change? Will you be able to get those leads with your current marketing processes? Will you need to hire more marketing people or outsource marketing? These are all ideas to explore while you do this exercise.

WHEN GROWTH BECOMES LETHAL: HIRING

What happens if you don't plan for growth? Fast growth can kill a company when companies hire as a reaction to growth without being strategic. Reactionary hiring can mean that you overspend on payroll, and even though you are growing your gross revenue number with increased sales, your profit margin will suffer if you are not careful.

Your hiring should be planned. Don't wait until you are understaffed and then hire in a hurry. Don't wait until you have outgrown your process, and instead of fixing a broken process, you just add more people. This will also affect the quality of the people you hire because you will be hiring out of desperation and are more apt to take anyone to fill a seat. You will hire in an unplanned way, just like the sprawling, unorganized home in chapter seven. Don't just slap on rooms haphazardly; create a blueprint for growth and follow it.

You will go through *fat* and *skinny* phases. Running fat means that when you are scaling for growth, you will hire some resources that you won't 100 percent utilize at first. You are ramping up for growth in this phase. Early on, we hired a dispatcher when we were averaging about thirty moves a day. Dispatching thirty moves a day didn't take much time so, at first, he had lots of free time on his hands. The cost per dispatching a move was his salary divided by the number of moves per year, which is a substantial number. Our dispatch labor cost per move was high—we were running fat.

Let's do the math, using round numbers and keeping it simple by not calculating for inflation and salary increases:

FAT	SKINNY	FAT
Year 1	Year 5	Year 6
Dispatcher salary: $50,000	Dispatcher salary: $50,000	2 Dispatcher salaries: $100,000
Moves dispatched per year: 10,950	Moves dispatched per year: 32,850	Moves dispatched per year: 36,135
Price to dispatch one move: $4.56	Price to dispatch one move: $1.52	Price to dispatch one move: $2.77

If a dispatcher costs $50,000 a year to dispatch 10,950 moves, it would cost $4.56 to dispatch each move. We would be running fat in that department.

Years later, the dispatcher is used at full capacity. To keep it simple, let's say we didn't give him a raise, and he was still making $50,000 a year and dispatching 32,850 moves. It would then only cost us $1.52 a move. Now we are running skinny.

As we grew and he dispatched more moves each day, we were able to reduce our dispatch cost per move because we could spread his salary over a greater number of dispatched moves. Now we decide that we need to add an additional dispatcher, and again you can see that we recognize the expense of an additional salary before we are able to keep the new person busy 100 percent of the time. The price per dispatched move increases to $2.77 a move. Now we are running fatter again. If growth happens then it is okay to have extra human resource capacity, but if there is a sudden decrease in moves we may need to let this person go.

You take a financial hit for a new salary before you reap the full benefits of a new hire. (This will create a J Curve, and we will learn more about that in the next section.) Let's look at hiring a new department manager. At first, the management cost is spread over the two or three people she manages, which initially is an inflated cost because the department that she is managing is small and her cost is spread over the few people she manages. You are running that department fat. Then you keep hiring people to grow the department, and soon the person is managing twelve people, and now you are running skinny because her cost is spread over twelve people. Let's look at another example. Say you add a controller or CFO to a $4 million company—that's a big expense. When the company grows to $8 million, the ratio of the controller's cost to the company's total revenue will be more in line.

You have to monitor ratios of each expense compared to the monthly revenue to keep your expenses in check so you don't run out of cash and so you have a healthy profit margin,. You should track the ratio of payroll, operating expenses, and other expenses as a percentage of your gross revenue number on a monthly basis. If, for example, your monthly payroll for your administration staff costs 10 percent of your gross revenue normally and suddenly you see it jump to 20 percent, this should be a red flag. If you are planning for growth and it readjusts itself when you ramp up, then that is OK. Your expenses should track your revenue to stay profitable. If the growth doesn't occur, then you need to reduce your expenses, or your profit margin will be negatively affected.

Here is a simple example of how to track these figures, using small round numbers to illustrate how you should monitor your expenses:

MONTH	January	% of Revenue	February	% of Revenue	March	% of Revenue
REVENUE	$1,000		$1,500		$500	
COST OF GOODS	$500	50%	$1,000	66%	$250	50%
PAYROLL	$100	10%	$150	10%	$200	40%

The two red flags in the above chart are the cost of goods for February. Why did they jump to 66 percent from 50 percent in January? COGs should be a consistent percentage of revenue. Also notice that the ratio of payroll to revenue is normally 10 percent. The company had an increase in revenue in February and hired more people. Unfortunately, March's numbers are low, and now the ratio of payroll to revenue is too high at 40 percent. If there are no new sales in your pipeline to grow your revenue, you will have to think about reducing your payroll to stay profitable.

It is OK to run fat while you are positioning your company for growth. Adding a new machine or ramping up staff in preparation for growth is necessary. However, if you hire without a plan and are not paying attention to your overhead, you can easily end the year with decreased profits, especially if there is a quick dip in the economy and you have hired too many people while expecting growth.

When an economic downturn happens, the business owner's attention often is immediately focused on the decrease in sales; the owner works hard to increase the sales number. Meanwhile, while the owner is preoccupied with keeping up with growth, she forgets that the company is running fat—the costs are too high for the amount of revenue the company is generating, which can place the company in danger of bankruptcy. A business owner needs to focus on sales while simultaneously readjusting from being a fat company poised for growth to a skinny company ready for a recession. It is financially dangerous to enter a recession with fat overhead.

In a perfect world, revenue and expenses would increase together, and the ratio between the revenue and expenses would be consistent. The economy, however, has cycles, so you have to monitor your expenses so that it tracks revenue. If you don't monitor your expenses, during an economic downturn your attention will be focused on trying to increase your sales—rather than focused on your high overhead, which could cause you to run out of cash.

When oil prices dropped in 2015, large Texas oil companies readjusted to prepare for the shortage in revenue. They had massive layoffs. Smaller oil field service companies who lacked the sophistication and resources went out of business. They had purchased more equipment and hired more people during the industry boom and were unable to readjust quickly enough during the bust. Equipment sat idle with notes that couldn't be paid back to the bank. Employees sat on the bench, burning through dwindling funds. Good-hearted small business owners don't have the stomach to lay people off like the large oil and gas companies until it's too late. In those cases, companies went under, and everyone was left unemployed.

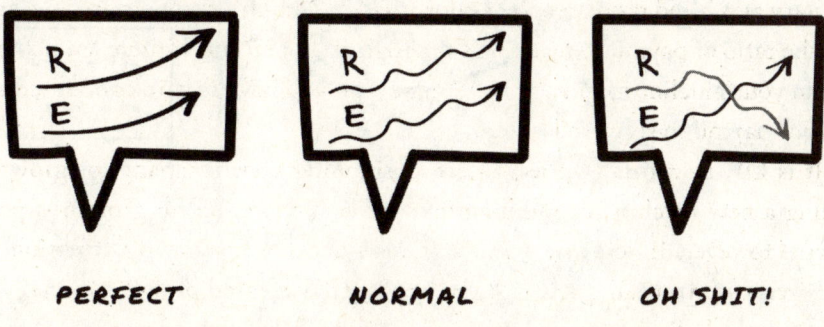

Your business's normal state should be to run on the skinny side. However, if you are expecting rampant growth, project that growth and allocate resources to ramp up. Run a little fat on your overhead in preparation for the growth. Monitor your growth, and if it doesn't happen, you may have to reduce your overhead or stop buying and hiring until revenue catches up with expenses.

Remember to always monitor your expense ratios and let your growth catch up with your overhead until you are balanced and skinny again before hiring more people.

MANAGING YOUR J CURVE

Nick Setchell, founder of RealTime CEO and a thought leader on financial modeling, introduced me to the J Curve concept, which is the same principle I was using in my fat and skinny theory, but Nick's way of explaining it is more analytical and elegant.

The J Curve runs along two axes: time and money. Anytime you spend money in a new way—for example, new software, a new hire, a new location, or when you introduce a new product or launch a new idea—a J Curve will

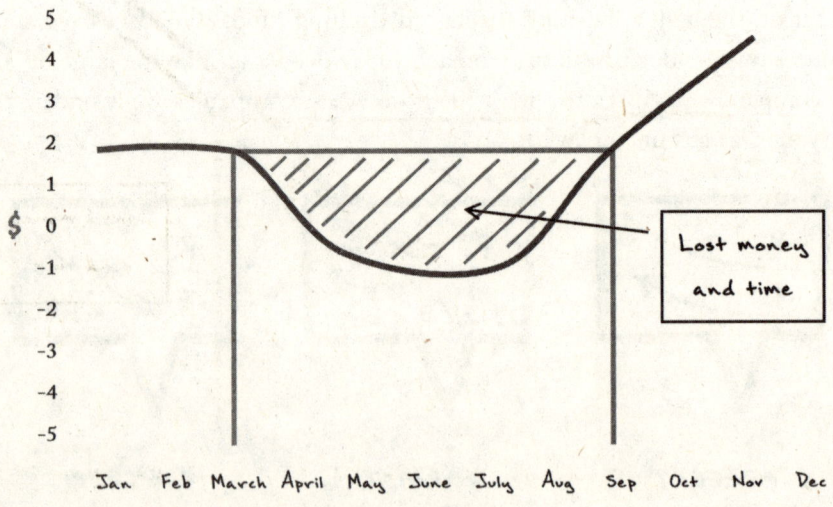

follow. When you make an investment to grow your company, immediately the expense will hit your financials, but normally you won't reap the financial benefit of the expense for some time. That creates a decrease in profits until your company realizes the benefits of the expense.

For example, suppose you hire a new salesperson in March. It takes him six months to ramp up sales to cover his base salary. The shaded area in the J Curve model is the money you lose.

What if you can decrease the J Curve by ramping up the time to have him hit his sales target in three months instead of six months? To do this, maybe you get him through training quicker or give him a list of prequalified leads instead of having him build his customer base through cold calling and prospecting. The area that is no longer shaded in the model is the money you will save by decreasing your J Curve (see below).

Think about companies like Uber and Lyft. Earlier, if a cab service wanted to add a taxi, someone would have to go out and purchase a car, get the logo installed, and then start interviewing drivers to drive that car. Now, potential drivers can log into an app, sign up, and start driving their own vehicle quickly. Uber managed to reduce the J Curve and friction to add vehicles, and this

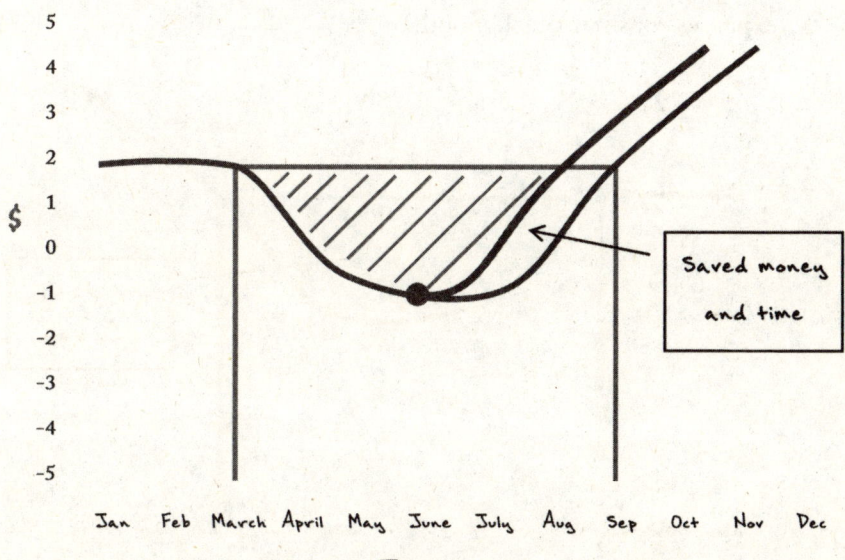

became a competitive advantage that aided its rapid growth. Companies who have nonlinear growth look for ways to reduce their J Curve.

What if you hire multiple salespeople at once and they all take six months to ramp up? This could be too many J Curves at once and severely affect your company's profitability. As a business owner, you need to identify and monitor all J Curves and try to reduce them whenever possible.

Don't take on too many J Curves at once, or you will run out of cash.

END OF CHAPTER CHECKLIST

- ❑ Identify possible J Curves. What creates them in your company?
- ❑ Are there ways you can reduce the depth or length of your J Curve and, by doing so, reduce either the cost or the duration of the J Curve?
- ❑ Work on creating a backcasting chart and see what areas you will need to add resources to in order to grow. Are there any ways to increase your efficiencies?
- ❑ Create an income statement (profit and loss statement) and create ratios for each expense to revenue. Example: Payroll is X percent of revenue. Do this monthly for a period of a few years and begin to notice patterns and if certain expenses are growing faster than your revenue. Are your expenses consistent each month?

END OF PART 2 CHECKLIST

- ❏ I have a mission statement that doesn't focus on money and gives my team purpose. It is our *Why*.
- ❏ I have asked, "Are we living up to [insert mission statement]?" in our daily decision-making.
- ❏ I have drawn out my company's workflow from beginning to end in a process chart.
- ❏ I have labeled the process chart with the job titles of those who work in each part of the process.
- ❏ I have circled processes that can be grouped together to create a department.
- ❏ I have added names of people who oversee each department. These people are ultimately accountable for everything in the part of the process they own.
- ❏ I have used my labeled process chart to draw an organizational chart.
- ❏ I have created and shared bullet-point job descriptions for every position within the business.
- ❏ I have created and shared a Decision Authority chart.
- ❏ I have looked at my process chart and added three or fewer KPIs for each department and for individuals, ensuring that I am only monitoring the most important things that are affecting business.
- ❏ I have created company-wide daily, weekly, and monthly key indicators and keep them in a location where the entire team can see our progress toward our goals.
- ❏ I have created a Backcasting Chart based on future projections and know how many people I will need in place to manage each stage of future growth. I also have analyzed processes, departments, equipment, and facility needs. I understand what resources our company needs in the next ten years, and I have started to make a plan to get a foundation established to meet the demands that growth will place on my business.
- ❏ I understand the concept of the J Curve and running fat or skinny. I monitor this monthly with an income statement and look at our expense line items as a ratio to our revenue. I make sure that the ratios

for any particular line stay in line with revenue. (For example, suppose my payroll is 25 percent of my monthly revenue on average. If it grows to 30 percent and we are heading into a recession, I will need to adjust.)

Note to Reader: You have finished Part 2, and by now you have created a scalable foundation for your business. When people talk about working *on* your business instead of *in* your business, the exercises you did at the end of each chapter are exactly what they are talking about. You have to take time away from your daily work to work at a strategic level to prepare your company and team for growth. With this planning, you have moved from reacting to growth in a rushed, haphazard way to being proactive and planning for growth. In Part 3, we will take strategy even further. We will talk about creating an accountable team. With an accountable team, you will be able to scale your business and achieve work-life balance for yourself and others.

Let's get off the hamster wheel and scale your company to the next level!

PART 3

Stop Holding People Accountable

11

Nature of Accountability

~~HOLDING~~ HIRING ACCOUNTABLE

Have you ever lain awake at night, thinking of a certain employee who wasn't performing up to your expectations? I know I have, and, unfortunately, I sometimes still do.

You find yourself having a mental conversation about how to convince this one person on your team to get their work done on time. You think,

> *Maybe I should have a heart-to-heart conversation with this person again and tell them about how everyone in the company is counting on them. Maybe I should write them up for their lack of action. What if I remind them daily or create a sign-off system for them, and if it isn't done, dock their pay? I could offer them an extra incentive plan so, if they start doing their work, they can receive a bonus.*

In frustration, your last thought is, *Maybe I should threaten to fire them!*

Here you are, losing valuable sleep, and thinking about begging, fining, bribing, and even threatening an employee to get them to do their job.

Thoughts You Have When You Have an Unaccountable Team
Heart-to-heart conversation: Begging
Dock their pay: Fining
Extra incentive: Bribing
Write them up/Fire them: Threatening

You think, "What is wrong with this underperformer?"

This underperformer is showing up day after day and is getting paid for not performing. If you are the one writing their paycheck and not getting the performance that your company needs, it doesn't seem like the employee is the one with issues.

If you are lying awake thinking about how to get someone to do their job, chances are you have the wrong person, and you need to fire them. Accountable people will be accountable with or without a bonus. You don't need to beg, bribe, or threaten accountable people. Accountable people are accountable. It is who they are—it is in their DNA.

When you have given an employee proper training and clear expectations of the results you expect and they are still not doing their work, it is time to let them go.

Once, I was asked why I don't "push" my people. I was told that I was too "nice" and I should be tougher. I don't like to "push" anyone, and my team doesn't like to be "pushed." Luckily, I don't have to push anyone at my office. If I am constantly pushing someone to get their work done, I have the wrong person. People will get their work done without any pushing if they are accountable. Accountable people push themselves. If you feel like the only way to get things done is by being tough on people, you have the wrong people.

Now let's look at the expression "Hold Accountable." The word *hold* means to grasp, carry, or support with one's arms or hands, while *accountable* means the willingness to accept responsibility or to account for one's actions. When placed together, the words conflict with each other: How can you support someone, *hold* them, while at the same time expecting them to be responsible for their own actions? If they were truly responsible, you would not have to *hold* them. When you hold someone accountable, you are taking accountability away from them.

Holding a team member accountable can be exhausting. Let's face it: Some people are not accountable no matter how hard you try to hold them. It is like hugging a seal: They always manage to slip through your arms.

UNACCOUNTABLE PEOPLE

People lack accountability for two reasons: They either lack *the will* to do their jobs or they lack *the skill*.

If they lack the will, it is an uphill battle trying to change them. Maybe they feel they are too good for the job and the work is beneath them. Maybe the relationship turned sideways somewhere along the way, and you can't get them back on track. Maybe their heart is elsewhere, and they are biding time in this position until their dream job comes along.

There is nothing worse than an employee who quits a job but doesn't give notice. They show up and collect their paycheck but have mentally checked out. Basically, they're just not that into you or your company, and most likely you know it, and everybody else does too.

If they lack the skill, you might be able to get them back on track if they have the aptitude to learn the skill. However, even with training, some people lack the appropriate aptitude.

Once I hired a friendly young woman to work in my Accounting department as a data entry clerk. She had one job, and that was to enter numbers into our software system quickly and accurately. Unfortunately, she was neither quick nor accurate. She did have other great skills, but data entry skills were not among them. Her manager was frustrated with her, and she was frustrated as well. The job wasn't for her, and, unfortunately, because my company was small at the time, I didn't have another position available that would be a good fit. I could have kept her and made her feel bad day after day for her lack of quality work, but I ended up letting her go. Though she certainly had the will, she did not have the required skill. While getting fired was painful, failing at her job every day also hurt, and I heard she got a new job that was people facing and her friendly personality helped her excel.

Forcing someone into a job that doesn't match their skill set is like entering a Shetland pony in the Kentucky Derby. It isn't that the Shetland pony is a bad horse; it's just the wrong horse for a contest involving speed.

THE NATURE OF ACCOUNTABILITY

Accountable people are accountable by nature. They will go over and around obstacles to get a task done, and you won't hear excuses from them. You don't have to bribe or threaten them. They are not Four-Forty-Fivers who watch the clock and start to pack up to leave every day at exactly 4:45 PM—they will stay a bit late if they are in the middle of something important. That is the way accountable people run.

Once an employee is trained and given the proper support and tools to do their job, they should *hold themselves* accountable with key indicators that you have set up for them.

You should not have to micromanage employees. Even new people on your team shouldn't be micromanaged: They should receive initial and ongoing training, but that is different than micromanaging. Micromanaging is stressful, and I can guarantee that neither you nor the person you are micromanaging will enjoy it—nobody likes it when people ride their ass.

People are happiest when they are working independently without a lot of control from their supervisors. Train them in their job, set key indicators to monitor your expectations, meet with them regularly to ensure they have the right tools they need to accomplish their work, and then get out of their way and let them work. If they can't work under these conditions, then you have the wrong person for your team.

Instead of trying to *hold people accountable*, try hiring *accountable people* and firing the ones who are not accountable.

Here are a few tips on what to ask and listen for during an interview to screen for accountable people:

- Ask about issues they may have encountered in a previous job and notice if they accept any blame for when things went wrong (e.g., "Tell me about a time when you missed a deadline"). Do they blame everyone else or accept accountability?
- If they don't accept any accountability, probe a little further with the question "Was there anything you could have done differently to have had a better outcome?"
- Ask about what they do personally to continue growing their work skills, such as which books they read, what courses they have taken.

- Ask specifically what they use to manage their calendars and work tasks. It doesn't matter whether they use a notebook or task software, just that they have a process in place.
- Ask about what happens when they lose focus and get off task, and how they get back on task.

If you ask a potential employee, "Are you accountable?" the obvious answer is a simple "Yes!" So, remember to ask open-ended questions that give them an opportunity to have long answers that allow you to get to know them better. Leave long silences after they answer your questions. Often after they have finished their polished, well-rehearsed answers, the good stuff comes from their attempt to fill the silence. Uncomfortable silences are great interview tactics. Embrace awkward silences; they are your friend.

While these interview tactics might help, remember that some people with low accountability might also have high bullshitting abilities, so a low-accountable person could still slip onto your team. Make sure you have KPIs set up to immediately show you when you have a low performer and act quickly to get them off your team.

END OF CHAPTER CHECKLIST

- ❑ How would you rate your current team when it comes to being accountable?
- ❑ How would you rate yourself on allowing your team to be accountable? Do you *hold* your team accountable, or do you let them hold themselves accountable? (In other words, are you micromanaging?)
- ❑ Do you have your KPIs set up for each person so that you monitor results instead of micromanaging activities?
- ❑ Review the accountability questions and add them to your interview process.
- ❑ Get comfortable with long silences. When people finish with their polished answer during an interview, they usually come up with a more honest answer if you allow them to do so.

12

Solo Accountable

When there is a lapse in accountability and the shit hits the fan in a company, the blame game starts. Marketing blames Sales, Sales blames Operations, Operations blames Sales, and Accounting blames everyone. When this occurs, it is time to learn the concept of Solo Accountable, which means making only *one person* accountable for a task or process, and thus ensuring overall accountability.

Practice Solo Accountable when you are assigning tasks, even if it is for a group project. Make only one person in the group accountable for the task as well as the consequences if the task isn't completed. If the task is too big for one person to accomplish, they can get help from team members; they can work in a group. However, there should only be one name in the spot that shows who "owns" the task. This cuts down on the blame game and accountability dilution.

Never assign a task with more than one person's name on it, even for something as benign as a task for two people on your team to meet so they can brainstorm an issue. Schedule the task of arranging the meeting to one person. This will prevent someone from waiting for the other person to make the first move and will close the accountability loop, helping to ensure that the blame game doesn't begin: "I thought *you* were going to email me and invite . . ."

CONNECT THE PROBLEM TO THE CONSEQUENCES

Steven Kerr, PhD, a professor at City University of New York, authored an article about rewarding A while hoping for B. This concept explains how we often set up reward systems that undermine our goal. An easy way to understand this concept is when a child throws a tantrum at a store because they want a toy. The parent wants the child to stop crying and breaks down and buys them the toy. The parent wanted silence, but the toy rewarded the tantrum, and you can be sure more tantrums will occur because children catch on quickly that the tantrum worked effectively in getting them what they wanted. Thus the parent rewards A, the tantrum, while hoping for B, silence.

In business, sometimes subtly and other times blatantly, we reward for A while hoping for B. For example, in my company we used to have a problem with Sales overbooking move jobs during our busy season. The consequence for the salesperson who overbooked was that they would potentially get an increase in their commission check if Operations managed to squeeze their job in and get it done. Therefore, salespeople were highly incentivized to overbook. The people in Operations, the customers, and the movers and packers were left with cleaning up the fallout.

The movers and packers ended up working late into the night, while the Operations people had to handle upset customers who were unhappy about reschedules and late arrivals. Sometimes, the Operations staff had to call the customers and reschedule their service entirely. Moving companies are notorious for being "bad guys," so when we called to tell customers that we were going to be late or needed to reschedule, they immediately began to distrust us, damaging our relationship before we even started the job. Late arrivals placed our movers in an uphill battle to gain the customers' trust, and overbooking directly worked against our mission statement to create loyal fans.

And where was our Sales team during all of this? They were sitting pretty with a big fat commission check. Overbooking was good for them.

We would discuss the situations with Sales, they would nod and agree, and at the end of the month, they would continue to overbook. Finally, we decided to make them Solo Accountable for this situation. Sales created the problem, so we began to pull a report showing the last jobs booked that put us over capacity and then had the offending salespeople call the customers to reschedule the services. Nobody likes upsetting a customer, and facing real consequences led Sales to immediately stop overbooking.

For process accountability, look back at the process chart you drew in chapter seven. Make sure that everyone owns part of the process. Analyze the process drawing from the moment your customer first interacts with your company and continue it through the entire process. At each point of the process, identify who is accountable for what. Have your team collaborate on this project. Make your process sufficiently tight and tied down to who does what with key indicators that measure performance so that there is no escaping accountability. Everyone should clearly understand the mission of the company, their department, and how they personally fit into the overall mission.

Make sure that an employee isn't rewarded for creating a bad experience for customers or their colleagues, or reducing the profitability of the company. Another classic example of rewarding A while expecting B is setting up sales incentives. If a salesperson low-bids a job, they will increase their chances of getting the contract, but the company will lose money.

When holding a manager accountable, never allow a manager to blame their direct reports for an issue. Ultimately, the manager is 100 percent responsible for everything their direct report does. When things are not getting done within their department or are being done incorrectly, the manager needs to look in the mirror and ask if they have the right person on their team. If they have the right person, has this person been trained correctly? Either way, the manager must take responsibility for problems with their direct reports. To do this, managers must have the authority to hire and fire their direct reports. If you force them to keep people they don't want on their team, you should not hold them responsible for any person's performance or their team's performance.

If you operate each department like small companies within your company and look at department managers as if they were owners of these small companies, your job as a business owner gets a lot easier. The result is you will achieve work-life balance because your managers own their departments and the problems within them. Your job turns into a supporting role, making sure your managers have the feedback and resources they need to become successful.

Once you have a team of highly accountable people, everything becomes easier and even fun. You can actually take a peaceful vacation without your employees calling you about something going wrong at the office.

END OF CHAPTER CHECKLIST

- ☐ Create a list of all your employees and grade them on a scale of 1–5 on their ability to work without supervision, with the higher number corresponding with greater levels of independence. If you have been operating in an asshole business structure, it might be difficult to know if they are able to work without supervision because you never gave them the opportunity to do so.
- ☐ Have critical conversations with those who have a low accountability score. Make sure they understand your expectations for their roles.
- ☐ Work with your employees to set reasonable key indicators for their position.
- ☐ Help employees understand their key indicators—what they mean and what is considered good performance. Get buy-in from them that these parameters are an acceptable measurement of a job well done.
- ☐ Start monitoring their key indicators and talk to them weekly so they understand where they meet or exceed expectations, and where they are falling short.
- ☐ Create a plan with them on how to improve where they are falling short.
- ☐ When you set performance expectations with KPIs, set a period of time that they will no longer be on the team if they can't reach the expectations for the position.
- ☐ Create a workflow chart and make sure a single person "owns" the success of each part of your workflow. No two people should own a single process.

Note: It is important to be empathetic. The reason you need to get someone off the team isn't because they are a bad person, but because their actions and abilities are not a good fit for the work you need them to do. It is hard for people to separate who they are from what they are capable of doing. They may be great employees but just not a fit for the job position or your company's culture. These employees may go on to find other jobs in which they become phenomenally successful because they are a better fit for a different environment.

13

When "Pretty Good" Is Bad

Words are important. Using the wrong words can diminish accountability on your team. To foster a culture of accountability in your business, you must understand the difference between *accountable* language and *unaccountable* language.

Unaccountable people tend not to give direct answers.

QUESTION: "Did you finish that project?"
ANSWERS: "Almost."
                "Pretty much."
                "Well, most of it."
                "Should be finished soon."
                "Any time now."

Any answer besides a "Yes" or "No" should raise an eyebrow. Even a "No" is more accountable than a "Yes, but" (my mentor once told me that the only thing that comes after a but[t] is a bunch of shit).

Many years ago, I bought my kids and nephew each a baby chick. My nephew accidentally killed his by petting it too hard. When I noticed the little chick lying lifeless in his hand, I knew something was wrong and asked him if the chick was dead. He nervously responded, "It is only a little dead." "A little dead" is equivalent to "Almost done." A job is either done or it isn't.

LOW-ACCOUNTABLE DETECTING

I have sat in on numerous meetings in other organizations and can tell immediately if a culture is accountable by the language people use during the meetings. Teach yourself to listen for and detect *low-accountable* words.

> QUESTION: "How did it work out?"
> ANSWER: "Pretty well." In other words, it worked out *less than well* or *not well at all*.

or

> QUESTION: "Can you get this done by Friday?"
> ANSWER: "I should be able to do that."

What does the answer exactly mean? The word *should* certainly indicates a lack of confidence. It is much different from a "Yes, I can get it done by Friday."

Replace words such as would, could, *and* should *with* can, will, *and* shall.

Modifiers—such as *pretty much, kind of, almost, really*—are words that lessen the action they are describing. These words move things into a gray area. "It's done" means that the task is complete. "It is *almost* done" means that the task isn't complete; the word *almost* moves *done* into a gray area.

If you want to detect when someone is lying or being deceptive, you will find that liars use an increased number of modifiers in their responses to direct questions. Modifiers soften the lie.

> QUESTION: "How do I look in this dress, honey?"
> ANSWER: "Pretty good," which means *not great*.
> QUESTION: "Does this dress make my ass look fat?"
> ANSWER: "Not really," which means it *really* does.

Unaccountable words also move you away from getting exact deadlines for projects. You will notice this during meetings in unaccountable work cultures.

QUESTION: "When will you be able to get this done?"
ANSWERS: "Soon."
"Next few days."
"Sometime next week."

An accountable answer would be "Next Wednesday by 5 PM."

I can tell if a company is accountable by listening for how, and if, they delegate tasks. During a meeting, if you bring up an action item and nobody writes it down with a deadline and a task owner, you are not holding a tactical meeting. Instead, you are holding a willy-nilly brainstorming session. All action items should be documented using the OCD method, discussed below, so that, at the end of each meeting, people will know what everyone is accountable for doing.

For example, when someone on your team says, "I think we should create a new process to fix this issue," ask, "Is this an action item?" Basically, you are asking whether this is something your team should invest time and resources to commit to doing. If the answer is yes, ask, "Are you going to own this?" and "When will it be completed?"

Other words to watch out for are descriptive adjectives such as *improve*, *increase*, *decrease*, *grow*, *shrink*, *enhance*, *better*, or basically any words that are not measurable. You need to add a number behind these adjectives. For example, a measurable action would be *improve gross revenue by 15 percent, shrink claims by 5 percent*. Without these numbers, it is difficult to understand if a person completed what they set out to do.

THE OCD METHOD

To properly execute a task, you must always document three things: owner, commitment, and deadline—this is the OCD method.

1. **Owner:** Who will own this job? Remember that, in Solo Accountable, only one person should be assigned a job. Several people can work on a task, but only one person's ass should be on the line if it doesn't get completed or completed well.

2. **Commitment:** What is the commitment? Define your task in a way that can be measured. Some types of jobs are definite, while other types of jobs must be measurable.

   A *definite task* would be getting a report finished or a marketing brochure done. This is like the baby chick. It is done or not done. There is no gray area.

   A *measurable task* would be to increase sales. But the word *increase* is ambiguous. If you increased sales by one cent, technically you would have achieved your goal. Instead of simply saying "increase," you would need to add by how much. *Improved sales* would not be a commitment, but *improved sales by 15 percent* would be a commitment.

3. **Deadline:** When will the job be complete? If you want a person to hold themselves accountable, then allow them to choose when they will complete their tasks. They know their workload, what they are capable of doing, and how fast they are able to get things done.

Resist the need to follow up with employees on the status of their tasks. Let them work autonomously until the deadlines. Offer help in the form of mentorship during their 1-2-1 meetings, and let them know that if they get stuck, they can come to you.

END OF CHAPTER CHECKLIST

Accountability Audit

- ☐ Do an Accountability Audit of your next meeting to determine whether your organization is using accountable or unaccountable language. Then, use your cell phone to record your next meeting. Later:
  — Listen for any idea that is brought up without an OCD.
  — Listen for *unaccountable* words.
  — Listen for unmeasurable goals.
- ☐ If you identity unaccountable language in your organization, call it out and make an effort to change. Start using accountable language and defining measurable goals.
- ☐ Stop assigning jobs to a group of people. Instead, ensure that each task has an owner who will be the person accountable for getting the job done.

14

Fire Top Performers

There's one decision that every business owner dreads, and it's not the decision about whether to raise or lower prices, buy new software, open a new location, or start a new product line. The most common challenge is whether to fire an underperforming employee. *Theresa in Accounting isn't getting our monthly numbers completed on time. How do I handle my Sales manager, Bob, who doesn't meet his sales goal and vanishes from the office every Friday afternoon? Is it time to fire my head of Operations?*

In Vistage, my business mentoring group, we have a mantra: *Hire slowly and fire fast.* We repeat this phrase all the time in the hope that one day it will sink in and become second nature. Yet the funny thing is that, no matter how many times we repeat it, we constantly process issues about employees who aren't good fits, and then process the same issue about the same employee a year later! We counsel our peers to let the problem employees go, yet they, and we, often keep the underperforming employees for an additional year.

Why don't we fire people who can't or won't do their jobs? We engage in magical thinking. We think, *Somehow, people will change and improve.* In reality, however, it is usually time to let them go.

We have many different ways to say *termination*: to make redundant; to let an employee realize their greatness elsewhere; to pink-slip, downsize, fire, let go—whatever you want to call it, it is by far the most painful part of my job. Its awfulness is no doubt connected to my need for acceptance, a need that is hardwired in many of our brains because, during our earliest days, membership in a tribe increased our chances of survival, and anyone ostracized or rejected from the tribe faced certain death, as I mentioned back in chapter five. It doesn't feel good to fire a team member and throw them out into the harsh, cruel world, and it certainly doesn't feel good to the employee who is getting fired.

Business owners agree that firing is one of the hardest things they do. No one likes to fire someone on their team. If you find someone who does, they are most likely a psychopath. Unfortunately, it is necessary to get rid of non-performers in order to create a high-performing team.

> **At the end of the day, you have the team that you are willing to put up with.**

If you are constantly saying, "This guy is an idiot!" about one of your teammates, who is the real idiot? The guy who shows up, does a substandard job, and still gets to earn a paycheck, or you, the person who allows him to do substandard work and is still paying him his wage?

Firing for Lack of Will: I don't get as stressed out when I have to fire an employee who is capable but is unwilling to do a good job due to a bad attitude. These people don't want to be a part of your organization anyway, so ultimately, they fire themselves. Usually, people with bad attitudes rub everyone on the team wrong, and their teammates are so happy when they leave that there is practically a party on their last day.

Firing for Lack of Skill: The difficult fires are the people on your team who the company has outgrown or who were bad hires in the first place. These are people who show up on time, who work hard and with enthusiasm, but simply are not capable of doing their job correctly, even with additional training. If your company is large enough, there are times you can move them to a different position, but sometimes you won't have a position available and you will just have to let them go. Letting go of individuals who lack the skill is heartbreaking, and I haven't found a way around not feeling like a jerk afterward.

When I first started with 3 Men Movers, I had a particularly difficult driver. He was not well groomed, did not maintain his truck, and showed up late to jobs. My dad used to say, "Show me a clean truck, and I will show you a good mover." You can tell a lot about movers by how they maintain their trucks. He had several family members working for the company, all of whom provided amazing service. He seemed protected from being terminated due to his family's connections and his seniority. He was, however, a customer service nightmare, so I canceled his contract.

I feared the backlash from this decision, but I knew it was the right thing to do. Would his family be upset? Would they leave because they thought I was unfair? A week later, one of his brothers-in-law, who was an excellent mover, came into my office and wanted to speak to me. I met with him, expecting the worst. Instead, he said, "We were all wondering why you didn't do it sooner."

> **Good people on your team recognize who the underperformers are, and they are wondering why you are keeping them around.**

The ironic thing about letting someone go is that, although I am riddled with anxiety prior to giving the person the news, I have never once regretted it afterward. Once the deed is done, I think, *Why the hell didn't I do that sooner?* Later, other people on my team will tell me they are happy that I finally got around to firing that person. Then they tell me horrible things that person was doing that I didn't even know about.

High performers don't want to work with people who don't care; they want to be around other serious high performers. It is demotivating when employees are doing everything right while their coworker is screwing around yet still getting paid. Allowing underperformers to remain on your team devalues the work your high performers are doing.

USE THE PEOPLE ASSESSMENT MATRIX

ATTITUDE

	HIGH	LOW
APTITUDE HIGH	The Golden Child	$ The Untouchable
APTITUDE LOW	♥ The Mascot	The Wrong Hire

Companies that are good at weeding out poor-performing employees and getting them quickly off their teams grow faster. Here is a way for you to assess your team and decide if an employee is a good fit for your company:

Look at the four quadrants in the above People Assessment Matrix and place the people on your team according to their attitude and aptitude.

Attitude Score measures how they show up mentally to work. A high score means they cause no drama and bring positive energy with them to work. If their attitude is low, it means they come to work with a bad attitude, create drama, and take away from the company's mission.

Aptitude Score measures if they have the ability to perform the tasks they're assigned in accordance with the company's standards. Simply put, do they do "good work"? (Keep in mind that they may be performing the task incorrectly if they did not receive proper training and communication. For the purpose of this exercise, we are going to assume that you have trained your staff properly and they understand what is expected from them.) If they have a high aptitude score, then they are accountable people who can get their work done without micromanaging. A low aptitude score means you can't count on them to get their job done.

Easy Decisions

Most leaders have an easy time deciding what to do with people on their team who fall into the following two categories:

1. **The Golden Child** (High Attitude/High Aptitude): These are your A-players. These folks hit their goals, have few excuses, and are cultural fits. To lead them, you make sure they have the tools they need to perform, are fairly compensated for their work, and then get out of their way. These are the folks whom you should mentor and invest time in—unfortunately, we tend to spend too much time on our problem employees and not enough time with our A-players growing the company.
2. **The Wrong Hire** (Low Attitude/Low Aptitude): Usually after the honeymoon period for a new hire wears off, you can tell right away whether you've made a bad hire. This person not only performs poorly but has a bad attitude too. People who fall into this category are easy to let go unless you are masochistic, or maybe you are so understaffed due to bad planning that any person with a pulse is better than an empty seat.

When It's Complicated

The other two quadrants are more challenging.

1. **The Untouchable** (Low Attitude/High Aptitude): This employee is a rock star when it comes to performance but is a nightmare when it comes to cultural fit. These people are usually high-drama rulebreakers. It's the top sales guy who doesn't show up for the mandatory sales meetings, or maybe the accountant who always closes the books on time but has a "Go Away!" sign on her door. Their peers don't like them, but they do such a good job hitting their goals that you are

reluctant to let them go. They might also be the person who knows all the unwritten processes, so by not having documented processes, you feel forced to keep them because nobody else knows how to do their job.

These people seem untouchable to their peers. Management seems to have a different set of rules for them because they are too valuable to the company. Even if they are good performers, you need to ask yourself if keeping them is detrimental to your entire company's culture. If you are honest with yourself, you know the answer: You must strategically fire The Untouchable. Everyone should share your company values, or they are not a good cultural fit.

2. **The Mascot** (High Attitude/Low Aptitude): These lovable humans are the office mascots. They show up on time every day and float around the office without contributing work that moves the company closer to reaching its vision. They are good people and well liked, but they don't get the job done. Maybe the company has outgrown them.

Ask yourself whether you are willing to lower the overall performance requirements so this person can do their job adequately. If you are willing to lower the bar so the employee meets the job requirements, then you can keep them on your payroll. And maybe, in some situations, you are justified in lowering that bar. Maybe an employee is going through a tough situation at home, and your team comes together and decides to lower the amount of output for this particular employee until things get better for them at home, or even indefinitely. If that is the case, acknowledge it and lower their key indicators so that they are able to hit the expectation you require for that position. There has to be a conscious decision to lower the bar—without it, you are allowing someone to underperform, which leads to the erosion of an accountable culture.

If you decide to lower someone's job requirements—unless this is a planned team decision—many times it doesn't work out. People on your team will begin to feel resentful for carrying this person's extra load. Once, we had a valuable member of our team who had a major health crisis, and it was going to take a long time for the employee to get back to full throttle. The issue was discussed, and the entire team made the unanimous decision to lower the bar and eagerly agreed to take up the slack until he could return to full duties.

If you are unwilling to lower the job's performance requirements, you need to fire The Mascot. Everyone deserves to feel successful in their line of work, and it is unfair to The Mascot to keep him in a position that doesn't lead to his success. If you have set clear expectations and have given him ample training and he still can't get his job done, let him have the opportunity to succeed elsewhere. It is harsh, but you are running a business, not a charity, and you need to fire him.

It is harder to make decisions about The Untouchable and The Mascot because they are not entirely bad. You will notice a dollar sign in The Untouchable quadrant and a heart in The Mascot quadrant. Financially motivated leaders look at how an employee affects the profitability of their company. These types of leaders will be reluctant to fire The Untouchable because they can't see beyond the revenue they hope this person will bring into the company.

Business leaders who make their decisions based on how they feel don't want to fire nice people, even if they are not performing. It is hard to see beyond the value of the nice person, even if they are not capable of getting the job that is expected of them done.

Leadership Styles

If you run a company with your heart, like I do, The Mascot will be a difficult termination. It is hard to fire a "nice person." But is it nice of me to keep a nice person in a job they suck at? Is it nice of me to prevent an employee from finding a job that's better suited to their talents and skills where they may have a better chance of achieving success and furthering their career? Everyone deserves the opportunity to feel successful, and if you have a great person who isn't a good fit, they deserve to know the truth so that they are able to find a different type of job.

One of my managers was a sweetheart. She was so nice that she let people on her team come and go as they pleased. This resulted in our office being understaffed and unable to help our customers efficiently. She was so nice that she helped individuals on her team succeed in a way that hurt the overall success of our company by doing things that helped increase a certain sales agent's closing rates, but it hurt the overall sales numbers for the company, and thus her key indicators for her job performance were always below standard. It was hard to fire this nice person, but it was necessary.

If you run your business based solely on profitability, The Untouchable will be a hard termination. It is difficult to fire a "top performer" who is a high contributor to your goals, but The Untouchable is a culture-destroyer who will ultimately hurt the profitability of the team. You may lose good employees who are unable to work with the drama The Untouchable brings to work. The drama might affect other people's performances, which will ultimately reduce the company's profitability.

While it is hard to fire people if, in your judgment, they are top performers, you may be measuring performance incorrectly. Performance should also be measured by the amount of drama and time it takes to manage The Untouchable. Performance should also be measured by the mood a person creates when they are employed by you. Do they bring energy and positivity to the team or do they drain the lifeblood out of everyone they are near? Do they share your company's core values? If they don't share your core values and you keep this person, then you need to change your core values. For example, if your written core value is *respect*, and you let a prima donna salesperson abuse your project manager, then *respect* isn't one of your core values. While the written core value is *respect*, the actual core value your company is practicing is *tyranny*.

I know of a businesswoman who had two top salespeople who were in The Untouchable quadrant. They were bringing in big numbers, so firing them would have hurt the company. She could tell that they were disengaged and actively hostile, yet she felt trapped in keeping them on her team because their sales numbers were good. Although she knew that they were not engaged, she didn't know that, instead of working on outside sales calls, they were actively working on starting their own company. They did all this while on her payroll. Not only did they set up their own company, but they also took several of her top clients with them when they left. If they had been fired when they first became disengaged, they might not have had the time and resources needed to start their own company that became a direct competitor to their former boss.

Ultimately, keeping The Untouchable is not in the best financial interest of your company.

NONPERFORMING ASSETS

People say that employees are your greatest assets and should be listed on your balance sheet. While I agree, I also believe that to improve the value of your company, you must sell off nonperforming assets. You only have a set amount of money to spend on payroll; therefore, you need to make sure you are getting the best employees you can get for what you are paying. Keeping nonperforming employees jeopardizes the profitability of the company and can ultimately hurt your entire workforce.

Think about your company like a helium balloon on a string tied to a brick. Your company wants to grow, and the helium is pulling the company up, but it can't rise into the air because it is tied to a brick. A nonperformer is like the brick at the end of the string. They prevent the company from growing. You have to cut the string to allow the balloon to rise.

Making the decision to terminate someone on your team is the hardest decision a leader will make. I challenge myself when I fire slowly and ask, *Why?* Allowing conflict to remain on your team will breed animosity on all sides. Why prolong the inevitable? Fire fast.

BULLSHIT REASONS

As leaders and business owners, we create a number of compelling bullshit reasons as to why we can't fire someone. Most of the time, a decision to keep someone on your team falls under one of three reasons: You're *lazy*, you're *chickenshit*, or you're *delusional*, each of which is reinforced by its own rationale.

YOU'RE LAZY

Rationale 1: *They know too much.* You don't have processes documented, and you dread taking the time to train someone else.

Rationale 2: *You don't have time to find or train a replacement.* You would rather spend your time doing something else that you deem more important.

When you look in the mirror, it comes down to being too lazy to start the hiring process. I get it! First, you have to kiss a bunch of frogs until you find the right person, and even then you won't be 100 percent sure they are the right person until you hire them and see how it works for a while. Let's face it: Hiring and training a new person when you are trying to grow your company is a pain in the ass.

YOU'RE CHICKENSHIT

Rationale 1: *What if you hire someone new, and they are worse than the person already in the position?* You are afraid of risk, and the known poor performer is better than the unknown who could be just as bad or even worse.

Rationale 2: *What if your employees are upset when you let this person go?* You are afraid of rejection and repercussions from your team.

Rationale 3: *The employee is mediocre, but if you hire someone new, it will take them months to ramp up, if they ever do.* You are afraid of lost profits and risk-averse to a J Curve dip when you hire someone new.

YOU'RE DELUSIONAL

Rationale: *You know that the employee hasn't figured out how to do their job so far, but, maybe by some miracle, it will sink in and the employee will start performing better in the future.*

I know from experience that to be good at answering incoming sales calls at my company takes less than a three-month learning curve, yet a year later, I will still hold on to a poor performer with hope that they may eventually catch on. But it has never happened! If they don't get it within three months of training, they never will. To think so is delusional.

Ask yourself a question that our guest speaker Hunter Lott asked my Vistage team: "Who on my team would I enthusiastically rehire?" Put a *yes* or *no* next to their name, then set about cleaning house. You owe nothing less to your A-players! They don't want to work with a bunch of incompetent people because you are too lazy, chickenshit, or delusional to make the tough call and remove them from your team.

Ouch, did that hurt? Yeah, I thought so!

END OF CHAPTER CHECKLIST

- ❑ Create a People Assessment Matrix and plot your current workforce.
- ❑ Identify your Mascots and Untouchables.
- ❑ Understand your reason for keeping Mascots and Untouchables on your team—are you chickenshit, lazy, or delusional?
- ❑ Create a plan to remove the Mascots and Untouchables from your team.
- ❑ Remember to be strategic about firing. You need to have a replacement ready when you fire a top performer. You also will need to have historical information that they know about your processes documented and ready for their replacement and be prepared for a dip in your J Curve.

15

Stop Helping

THE FIXER

Chances are you got into business because you are intelligent and are good at solving problems. As a business owner, you get to practice making big decisions every day, ensuring you become even better at it. You are the fixer within your organization. Your teammates come to you to ask for your help when making decisions, and why not? You excel at deciding. When there is an issue, you solve it with a quick solution, a *yes* or *no*, with no need to explain the decision.

I bet you even like to be the "go-to" person. I know I do. It is both challenging and fun to be in the center and fielding questions all day. It is great being the person with all the answers. Not only does it build your ego, but it feels *helpful*.

For your employees, it is good for them to have you make all the decisions. Not only do they get to push the problem-solving onto you, if something goes wrong, it will be your fault. In the long run, it is much safer if employees bring an issue to you because it obsolves them from any possible fallout from a poor decision.

When you make all the decisions, you feel needed and competent because everyone goes to you when they need help and, in turn, your team doesn't have to work hard to figure out solutions or be accountable for the results. When you think about it, it is a win-win, except if your plan is to grow your company.

AVOID THE ASSHOLE STRUCTURE

For a small company, centralized authority, where the owner has all the power, is common. You can run a small business with *you* in the center and with each employee running to you to help them make decisions. In a hospital emergency room, you need this type of decision-making. There is no time for getting buy-in from your team and fostering leadership growth. The doctor in charge, working with a small group, has total control, delivering orders that the staff obeys. If you decide to run your company in this manner, however, eventually you will limit its growth potential so that it never matures into a large company.

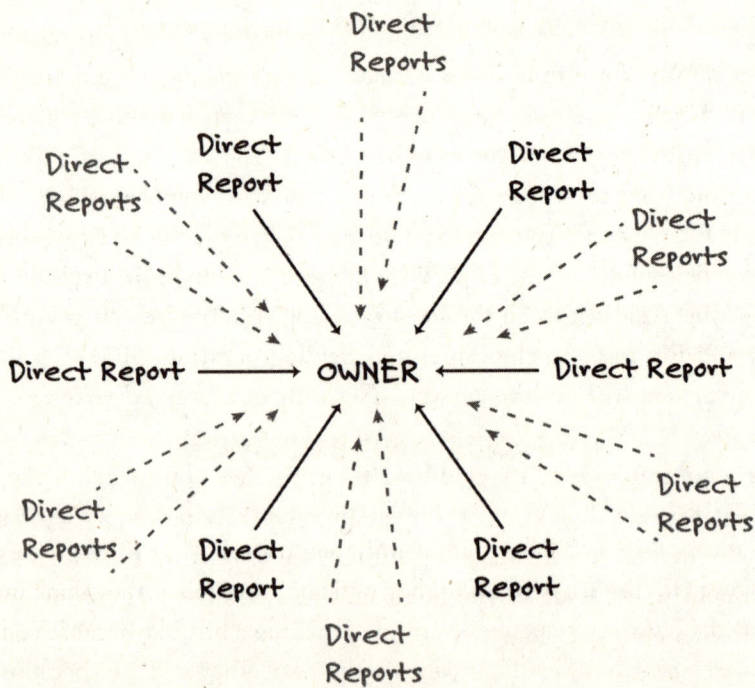

NONSCALABLE DIRECT REPORT STRUCTURE

When you solve problems for employees, you are robbing them of the chance to learn and grow their own decision-making and leadership abilities. To gain leadership skills, your people need to learn how to find viable solutions on their own and have the bravery to act on these solutions. The only way they will improve at making decisions is by practicing making decisions on their own.

Ultimately, you should want your people to be able to operate on their own—if they can't, you will not be able to scale your organization. Think about large companies. Do you think Sam Walton of Walmart needed to be involved in a decision to fire someone in another state? No, because he managed to build a culture that had processes in place and empowered managers to operate on their own.

There was a large furniture company located in Houston years ago that was phenomenally successful. The owner of the company ran it with an iron fist. Everything went through him. Unfortunately, he passed away, and shortly thereafter, the company went bankrupt. He had not built a company with structure and leadership that could carry on after his death. Ask yourself how long your company would be able to operate if you were to stop coming into the office tomorrow.

What if sporting events were run using an asshole structure? The quarterback has the ball. He is running, and he looks to throw the ball to the wide receiver. *Time-out.* He has to ask the coach whether he should throw the ball or instead try to run it down the field. Crazy, right? It doesn't happen that way because the coach has trained the quarterback on what to do in certain situations. He trusts the quarterback to make the decision on the fly—otherwise, the game would come to a halt.

UNHOOK AND EMPOWER

If you are the leader whose cell phone is ringing off the hook with your direct reports asking for your help, there is only one reason: Your direct reports are not empowered. They may feel like they will get in trouble if they don't include you in every decision. They may be afraid of making a mistake because you have gotten angry for mistakes they made in the past. They call you because they know you are going to tell them what to do.

You need to start pushing back on your team so they solve issues on their own.

If you have done the work from the previous chapters, you have already created a chart with job descriptions in bullet form for each individual within your organization. In chapter eight, you completed a Decision Authority exercise to address the most common decisions your people will come across and how they will handle these decisions. You are now ready for the next step to create an accountable culture, and that is shutting down the answering booth and opening up mentorships to build leadership within your organization. To start, you must teach your future leaders how to make good decisions.

Now, when they come to ask you to solve their problems, respond by asking them what they think they should do and then stay quiet. Remember, awkward silence is your friend. If your team is not used to this, they might try to push back and wait for you to solve their problems. Keep pushing the decision back to them. When they come up with a solution, you should then ask, "Why did you make this decision?" Give them a chance to articulate their decision-making process so they can solidify *why* they are making the decisions they are making. You want them to make purposeful, well-thought-out decisions.

If they come back with something you don't agree with, say to them, "Walk me through that." Let them articulate why they came up with the idea and how they think things will work out, then give them feedback. Ask them questions that might help them make a better decision.

Since I started doing this, I have noticed that even when I don't agree with my employee's decision at first, after they explain the reason behind why they made their decision, I often change my mind. Many times, I am not in the trenches and don't have all the information they are privy to. In these situations, I would have made a different decision and one that wasn't the best for the company. I have learned a lot from keeping my mouth shut and listening to team members walk me through their issues and their solutions. When I am running my mouth, I am not learning anything new. When I listen to my team, I am learning.

Even if you don't agree with the direction your employees want to take, if they are passionate about it, let them carry on with doing it their way. Sometimes you even need to let them fail. I know this can be challenging. Obviously, if it will adversely affect your profits, create legal problems, or hurt your culture or customer service, you can't let them fail. However, in other situations, if employees are passionate about a situation, let them see it through. How can you expect your managers to be accountable for their goals if they are not allowed to make big decisions?

IT DIDN'T WORK—YET

In order to create a safe place for your team to make decisions, you have to have a culture where your team feels safe enough to take risks. It is only called a *risk* if there is a chance of failure. If there isn't, it is called a *sure thing*. Many people tout themselves and their company as "risk-takers." *Risk-taking* is sexy. *Failure?* Not so much. If you want to foster a culture of innovation, you must not only embrace risk-taking but also embrace failure. Failure is the part that you don't often see, but it is what innovation is built on.

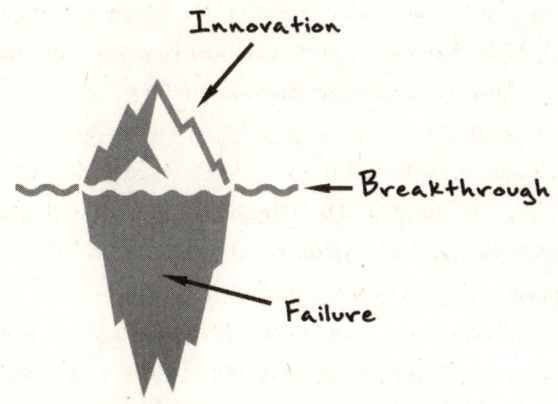

INNOVATION ICEBERG

How do you create a culture that is accepting of failure? When your department or someone on your team fails due to a wrong decision, you must not react with anger. You can feel disappointed, but never feel anger unless the failure is from lack of trying or laziness. The more risks your team takes, the greater the chance of failure. Instead of looking at it as "It didn't work," look at it as, "It didn't work—yet."

If a person on your team makes a decision that doesn't work out, and you become irritable and angry, you will shut them down from making future decisions. Also, you will create a culture of hiding mistakes, which can have a devastating long-term effect on the overall growth of your company. Mistakes should be transparent and communicated with the entire team so that your company can learn and grow from them. If they are hidden, you are bound to keep making the same mistakes over and over again.

I don't know of any employee who wakes up in the morning and thinks,

> *Today is the day! I am going to get to work and screw some shit up. I am going to make costly mistakes that I know will really piss off my boss and embarrass myself in front of my team. Then I am going to miss my numbers and let everyone down. I live for public humiliation and disappointing people.*

For the most part, people want to do well. Yet, even though we know that employees don't make conscious decisions to make mistakes, why is it that, when they do, we get upset with them?

As leaders, we need to be kinder and gentler with employees. They are trying the best they can. If we have already done the work to ensure that we only have A-players on our team, then isn't a mistake from an A-player OK? A-players don't want to fail, so if they make a mistake, the mistake itself is punishment enough. We don't need to pile on.

As leaders, if we allow poor performers to stay on our team, that is our fault, not the person who can't perform.

I know someone who runs a large manufacturing plant. He is a hell of a nice guy, but when someone on his team makes a mistake, he lets them have it. I am not sure if he vents out of frustration or if he believes that yelling at his team will teach them a lesson and thus they will not make the same mistake again. Either way, the yelling doesn't solve the issue and instead creates a culture of fear and people who cover up their mistakes.

MISTAKE SAFETY

When people make mistakes, you should let them know, but in doing so, you shouldn't shut them down from taking risks in the future. Instead, make sure that they feel safe to be vulnerable in order to tell you when something isn't working. Maybe a process needs to be changed, or something went wrong and your teammate needs support to fix the problem. If you shut your team down, they will hide their mistakes, and without transparency, your company will not be able to learn and grow.

One of my Vistage friends, Stephen King, has a board in his office that reads, *Celebrate Your Mistakes*. Employees are encouraged to publicize their mistakes to the whole company. They write out what went wrong on a notecard and include what they learned. Other employees can read the notecards and learn how to avoid mistakes in the future.

Leaders forget about what it's like to have a boss. When an employee goes home at night, *you* become their topic of dinnertime discussions. What will your employees say about you? Will it be this?

"How was your day, honey?"

"Well, I did all this work, and there was a mistake. I was hoping my boss wouldn't find out, but he did. Completely blew up at me in front of the team! It was so humiliating. I hate my job sometimes. My boss is an asshole."

Or will it be this?

"How was your day, honey?"

"Well, I found a mistake in the work I was doing today, and I shared it with my boss, and he put me in charge of creating a new process to make sure the same mistake doesn't happen to others. I think this will really add value to the company. We are thinking about completely changing our process, and overall, it will make the customers happier and save the company money. I love my job!"

Same company. Same mistake. Different culture. In the first scenario, you have a company that punishes mistakes, and in the second scenario you have a company that understands that mistakes are a part of growth and embraces mistakes as a learning opportunity.

The only mistake that should be unforgivable—and it isn't really a "mistake" at all—is an ethical violation of your values. One of our employees had trouble learning how to move furniture. He kept dropping things and causing damage. He was a great guy, but just had a long learning curve. We paid the damages and stuck with him, and he ended up being a great mover. On the other hand, another employee pocketed a fee that was supposed to be split between him and the company. It was only $40 and much less than what the first employee cost the company in damages. The thief was terminated immediately. Your company should have zero tolerance for ethical violations. A lapse in moral conduct is not the same as a mistake.

Managers must become good decision-makers. Don't rob them of the chance. Instead of coming to their aid and solving their problems, teach them how to solve them on their own. Without a self-sufficient team, you will never have a work-life balance. Your team will be reliant on your help to bail them out and fix problems. If they are insecure about their decision-making skills, they will need your blessing and approval on every issue.

It is understandable that, when you own your own business, you are on call 24/7, but most things should be able to wait until you get into the office. Most of the time, written processes can help your team make decisions, but there are always issues that come up that processes don't cover. In these cases, your team should make the best decision they can based on the company's core values.

Don't run an organization that puts you in the center and turns you into that asshole who must sign off on every little decision. Some owners like the feeling of control and need to be the center of a wheel. When people come to them for every little thing, it fills a need to feel important. However, if you want work-life balance, you need to have confident decision-makers who can take charge when you're not around, which lets you spend quality time with your family. When a business owner can't take a day off or get through their meal without a work-related call, it is a telltale sign that they have work to do in empowering decision-makers in the company.

Business owners sometimes are too afraid that their employees won't get it right. "I know if I do it myself, I won't make mistakes." You might be right. You can do lots of the jobs better than your employees and limit the mistakes that are made, but in doing so you will limit your company's growth.

Owners of the largest businesses have the most peace during their off-time. Logic would tell you that the bigger the company is, the more problems an owner will have, yet this isn't the case. Owners of billion-dollar companies are on yachts in the Mediterranean. The reason large companies can scale in the first place is that they have built leaders and structures within their organizations. Again, an empowered team is the biggest stress reliever. Make sure to pull yourself out of the middle, stop being that asshole, and align yourself in the circle with your team. Instead of you being in the middle, replace yourself with the company's mission and vision. That is effective leadership.

LISTEN. NO, REALLY LISTEN

Remember, when someone comes to you with a question, push back. Answer them with another question: "What do you think you should do?" Request more details: "Walk me through why you made that decision." And when someone tells you something that you don't believe, don't go into "that isn't right" mode and start defending your beliefs.

You must truly listen when your team speaks to you. That doesn't mean concocting your response in your head while you stare at them, pretending to listen. The concept of listening seems easy, but it is a hard skill to master.

When someone tells you something that seems crazy, don't cut them off. Even if what they say seems 100 percent wrong, resist telling them. If you do cut them off, you will end the conversation and the opportunity to change their mind. Ask them why they feel the way they do. Try to open a dialogue for understanding.

If your spouse says, "You don't love me," or your kids say, "You're unfair," or your employees say, "It wasn't my fault," don't shut down the dialogue by getting defensive and saying, "That's crazy" or "That isn't true." Instead, ask, "Why? What makes you say that?" and listen. Having a knee-jerk reaction and cutting someone off doesn't normally solve the problem. Have you ever told your spouse they were overreacting and they said, "Yeah, you're right about that!" Or your kids that it "*was* fair" and they agreed with you?

Listen and ask questions to understand where employees are coming from, as well as to foster a relationship based on trust and open communication.

END OF CHAPTER CHECKLIST

- ❏ I have a weekly 1-2-1 scheduled with each of my direct reports so they have a designated time to ask me questions.
- ❏ I have considered whether my reactions to mistakes might affect my team's willingness to make mistakes.
- ❏ I am going to work on not being an answering booth, and instead I am going to mentor my people to make decisions on their own and become the future leaders of my company.

16

Focus on Demotivating Employees

When my dad started in the Kirby business in the 1970s, he used to listen to motivational cassette tapes by Paul J. Meyer from the Success Motivation Institute while driving his big silver Buick. These tapes were all the rage for salespeople at the time, with titles such as *The Basic Factors for Success*, *How to Achieve Success*, *How to Develop a Positive Mental Attitude*, *How to Influence Others to Do What You Want Them To*, and *How to Develop a Winning Personality*. He believed that you could motivate people and get them "fired up" so that they, too, would become successful. He would drive down the country roads through the cornfields of Illinois to sales appointments and play positive-thinking cassette tapes at full volume. He would shout at the top of his lungs, "Act enthusiastic, and you will be enthusiastic!" Then he might howl like a wolf.

When we moved to Houston, he continued howling at night. One day a neighbor kid came up to me at the bus stop: "My parents want to know what all the howling noises were about coming from your place last night." I turned red with embarrassment. Needless to say, life with my dad was never boring.

My dad channeled his enthusiasm to keep his team motivated. While you can motivate people, motivation is short-lived unless people are intrinsically motivated. People who are intrinsically motivated will push on regardless of the external motivation they receive from management. You can become a cheerleader for your company and increase their drive; however, the easiest way to have a motivated team is to hire people who already have a great attitude. While it is hard to motivate people who don't have intrinsic motivation already, it is easy to demotivate a motivated person.

EIGHT WAYS TO DEMOTIVATE YOUR TEAM

It is an uphill battle to change just one person who has a negative attitude into someone with a positive attitude, but it is easy for a leader to *demotivate* an entire team. A negative attitude is like a cold: It's contagious. It can infect the whole company and decrease the overall morale of your team, so it is important that as a leader you stay positive and avoid behavior that can demotivate your team.

Here are eight ways you can demotivate your team:

1. **Keep an asshole for a manager or coworker.** No matter how much money that prima donna sales guy makes for you, if he is an asshole to his teammates, fire him. The same holds true for all of your managers. The asshole might be hitting their numbers, but the negative effects to the overall team can hurt, not only your company's morale, but its profits too. Remember: Get rid of The Untouchables.
2. **Don't pay fairly.** In the famous words of my first business mentor, Bill Peery, "Don't fuck with a man's paycheck." Pay on time, pay market rate or above, and don't nickel-and-dime. There is nothing worse for motivation than not being paid for the work you are doing. If there is confusion about commission or payroll, just eat the loss and pay what your employee expected. Payroll issues can simmer forever in an employee's brain and result in decreased performance, which equates to decreased profits. The overall loss due to decreased productivity from a disgruntled employee will far outweigh most paycheck disagreements.
3. **Overwork your team.** The job should be challenging, but not back-breaking. Yes, work is important, but keep it real. Occasionally, projects and deadlines might mean some late nights and weekends, but this shouldn't be the norm. People only have one chance to see their five-year-old graduate from kindergarten. Respect their commitments

to their family. Men especially are shamed for wanting to be involved with their kids. They shouldn't have to choose between being a dedicated father and a dedicated employee.

4. **Don't care.** Yeah, it sounds obvious, but people can tell if you care about them or if you are just going through the motions. When you ask them how their day was going, did you move on when they said, "Fine," or did you go deeper? If you really cared, you would ask open-ended questions and follow them up with a few more questions. "Did you do anything fun this weekend?" "Really? Tell me more."
5. **Micromanage.** A competent person doesn't want a manager who "rides their ass" all day. You should only have competent people on your team, so micromanaging should not be necessary.
6. **Don't communicate.** Your team wants to know what is going on with their performance and the company's performance. They want to understand what is required of them. You need to communicate those things consistently and clearly.
7. **Don't offer career paths.** Most people want opportunities for advancement. Just recently we were discussing an employee who seemed stuck for years. He was in a rut, and I made a note in my journal to take him to lunch and talk with him about where he was professionally and where he wanted to go. But I got busy (yes, that is a lame excuse), and didn't get around to going to lunch with him. I woke up one morning to an email from him giving me two weeks' notice. Did he move on to a superior opportunity, one that was either more challenging or paid better, or maybe both?
8. **Shut down your team's ideas.** Employees who are willing to share ideas are giving you a gift. Most don't. Most keep their mouths shut even if they think they have a promising idea because they have worked in "keep your head down and mouth shut and keep working" environments. When they give you this gift, stay open and receptive, regardless of how you feel about the idea, because if you don't, you might not just be shutting down the idea, but shutting down the person behind the idea.

Your team doesn't want much. They don't need free trips, gourmet lunches, and yoga classes. While all of these things add value, what they really want is an honest paycheck that is decent enough to take care of their family, a purpose for showing up to work, and respect.

In return, here is a checklist of what I expect from my team (and what you can expect from yours):

- ❏ **I expect my employees to fail.** If they are not making mistakes, they are playing it too safe and not innovating. If they don't tell me about their mistakes, we can't improve our processes and learn.
- ❏ **I expect my employees to call me on my shit and tell me "No."** I am a visionary and a pusher, and I need people around me to keep me in check sometimes.
- ❏ **I expect my employees to have "off" days.** Long-term employment is like a long-term marriage: You can't be "on" 100 percent of the time. I expect employees to communicate with me so I can take the pressure off them when they are "not feeling it."
- ❏ **I expect my employees to break policies.** When a policy gets in the way of customer service, our values, or our mission ("Create loyal fans one move at a time")—then maybe we need to bend the rules.
- ❏ **I expect my employees to get off task and goof around.** If I do not hear laughter on the floor or see goofy memes and gifs in our online chat, I worry about our culture.
- ❏ **I expect my employees to leave or push people out.** People talk about how their culture is a magnet and attracts the best people. Like a magnet, a strong company culture should also repel people who do not fit. People who are not talented, passionate, kind, and hardworking stick out and don't last.
- ❏ **I expect my employees to not follow their job description.** They should go beyond it and do whatever is ethically and legally possible to reach our goals and please our customers.
- ❏ **I expect that they will not always make the customer happy.** Yes, that is our number one goal, but we're not tacos: We can't make everyone happy. Some people you just can't make happy. Our employees come first, and sometimes we have to refuse a job if a customer is abusive, because we put our people over profits.
- ❏ **I expect my employees to not make work their top priority.** They should always put their family and their health first. We have a strong

team and can pick up the slack if someone has an emergency or even if they just want to make it to a Little League game.
- **I expect my employees to not focus on profits and the bottom line.** They should focus on creating value for our contractors and our customers. Profits are a result of reaching our goal, and our goal is to go beyond for our customers and contractors.

END OF CHAPTER CHECKLIST

- Think about your current employees. Which of them are internally motivated? Internally motivated employees are the ones who will be accountable for their work, while employees who lack internal motivation might not be worth the effort to keep on your team. You need to decide.
- Do you have any Four-Forty-Fivers—the ones who are just working for a paycheck and biding their time until they get off work? Would you be able to reignite and re-engage these folks? How?
- Review the eight ways to demotivate your team and be honest. Is your company doing anything that might demotivate an employee?
- What expectations do you have for your employees? Employees need to understand what your expectations are for them. Have your expectations been communicated to your team? Are they written down?

17

Fragile—Handle with Care

I was invited to a CEO lunch for Houston's executives. I was excited to receive the invite, despite the fact that the guest speaker was Bum Phillips. For those of you who are not football fans from Texas, which I am not, Bum Phillips was a Houston Oilers coach back in the day before the Oilers were hijacked from our state. He is a local legend.

Although Bum was beloved by most Houston football fans for his authenticity, his big heart, and the love he had for his players, I had seen Bum on TV and was underwhelmed. Bum was short and chubby, wore a huge cowboy hat, and spoke with a slow, thick southern drawl. He was a Texas hero, but I failed to see the attraction. I mean, really, what could I learn about business from a football coach?

Bum came out onstage in front of Houston's top executives to give his speech, and he was wearing his usual western attire amidst a sea of dark executive suits. His first words were disarming: "I don't know why dey ask me, a lil ole football coach, to come out hur today and speak with y'all about bidness." Well, I certainly agreed with him, but I had to smile. He knew his audience. What could he teach us? He segued immediately into a personal story.

While he was a football coach for the Oilers, he had a receiver who could not catch the ball. The receiver's only job was to catch the ball, and he couldn't do it. This was during training camp, and although Bum liked the kid, he was going to have to cut him from the team. Up until then, Bum had pulled him off to the side after each failed attempt and basically chastised him for doing a poor job. Bum would yell, "Catch the damn ball, son! Catch the goddamn ball!"

Bum finally made the decision that no amount of chewing out was going to get this young kid to perform better, and he would have to let him go. The decision was already made, but then Bum had an idea that he thought it couldn't hurt to try—after all, what did he have to lose? When the kid reached up for the ball and inevitably missed it, as he had hundreds of times before, instead of ripping him a new one, Bum said, "Dat a boy, you almost had it!" The kid, who by now could see the writing on the wall that his NFL hopes were flying out the window, at that moment had been given a glimmer of hope from his coach. Instead of being shut down in frustration from failure, he tried a little harder.

Again, he didn't catch the ball, but still Bum kept on telling him he was doing well and almost had it. This went on for weeks, and finally, the kid started making progress. His confidence began to soar, and as it did, he tried harder and harder, and he ended up staying on the team and becoming a huge contributor. Bum's story was about the importance of little wins.

After meeting Bum, I had to give it to him. I learned that day that there was quite a bit a football coach could teach to a group of executives.

THE EMPLOYEE'S NEEDS TRIANGLE

People are more fragile than we realize, and they place a huge amount of credibility in the feedback they get from their leaders. When they propose an idea, they are opening themselves up to being vulnerable, and how you receive their ideas can either motivate them or shut them down. If they complete a project that they have been toiling on for weeks, how much traction will you get from pointing out a little thing that *you* might have done slightly different? Employees who are pumped up and who feel like heroes will become heroes. Employees who are beat up on will shut down, and you will not get decent work from a dejected employee.

If 98 percent of your feedback is correcting employees or being negative, then why should they even try anymore? You begin to sound like background music, and an unpleasant song at that. However, if you spend 98 percent of the time building them up, then when they do hear anything critical, they will take notice.

My dad wasn't good at giving positive feedback. One time my mom cooked a new dish from a recipe she found in a newspaper, and my dad ate his dinner and never mentioned a thing. She was hurt and decided to push him a little to get some positive feedback. "I cooked a new recipe. Do you like it?" He responded, "Shirley, I expect everything you cook to taste good. If I don't like it, I will let you know."

When I started leading my team, I didn't give much praise. I learned from my dad that things should go well, and if they didn't, I would let them know, right? My mom didn't like only hearing feedback when things were going wrong, and neither did my team. I tried to get away with being this way by making the excuse that I was an introvert. It is true—I am—but I owe it to my team to let them know that I appreciate them.

I also struggled at giving positive feedback to my kids. I felt like it was my duty as a parent to help them be the best they could be. When my daughter asked me if I liked her drawing, I would respond, "It looks great, sweetie, but you should maybe add a bit more color to the sky." It was never, "It looks great." I didn't notice I was making them feel like nothing was ever good enough until my husband, John, said, "You can stop with 'It looks great.'"

Bill Peery, my mentor, showed me the Employee's Needs Triangle, which can help us understand what employees need if we want them to stay and feel happy and engaged.

- **Competent:** An employee needs to feel competent. If you are patronizing and the feedback you give them makes them feel stupid, then this need is not being met. Nobody on your team should be made to feel stupid. If they just can't get how to do their job, you either have the wrong person or you haven't trained them. Either way, it is your fault.
- **Safe:** An employee needs to feel like they have job security. They should not have to work in an environment in which they feel like at any moment they are going to get fired. Granted that sometimes you will need to let an employee go, but this shouldn't drag on for months. What is the point of an employee trying to improve their work if at

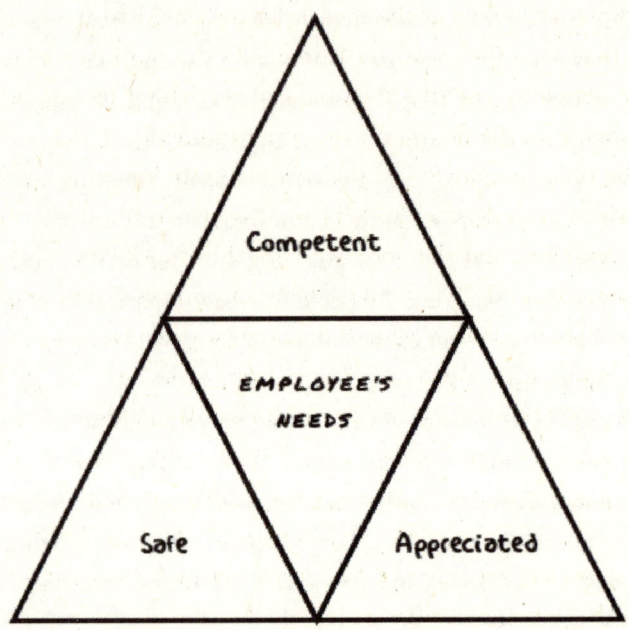

any minute they are waiting for a tap on the shoulder saying they are being terminated?
- **Appreciated:** An employee needs to feel that their work is appreciated both through actions and financial compensation. If an employee feels like they are being taken for granted, they will be unhappy and leave, or worse yet, stay and become disengaged.

If as an employer you are incapable of ensuring that these three needs are met, then most likely your employee will quit, either by walking out the door or by just mentally checking out. Every employee deserves to have these needs met, and if you can't meet these needs, you should quit torturing your poor employee and fire them. Keeping them and making them feel unsafe, stupid, or unappreciated at work is cruel.

When my dad had a stroke in 2002, he left the day-to-day operations to a manager who did not understand the importance of appreciating the workers out in the field. The office workers treated the movers and packers who did the manual labor as inferior. My father became a mover when he was fifty years old; he worked long hours, weekends, and did backbreaking work in the Houston heat. His work had value. I understood that to improve our work culture, our mindset of how we looked at the movers in the field had to change. We must understand that the office workers worked *for* the movers, not the other way around. The people in the office should do everything to support the movers while they are out in the field servicing our customers.

I saw the office employees as the cornerman in a boxing match. We were the people who squirted water in their mouths, wiped the sweat off them, massaged their shoulders, and shouted, "You got this!" and then pushed them back into the ring for Round Two. Under no circumstances were the office workers allowed to be rude or disrespectful to the movers. Then we took it a step further and put our movers on a pedestal: These guys were our heroes. We pumped them up and gave them a sense of pride in how well they worked and how much our customers raved about them.

When you are placed on a pedestal, the last thing you want to do is fall off. If they receive a negative review, our movers are devastated. They care deeply about their superhero reputations. When we have new hires in our Operations department, the learning curve is always about how to approach bad reviews. It takes them a few weeks to realize that it is unnecessary to discipline the drivers for bad reviews because the drivers are already harder on themselves than anyone else would need to be. Bad reviews crush them.

In 2004, we received a call from Cycle, formerly known as Elves & More, an organization that has given away thousands of bikes to underprivileged local schoolchildren during the Christmas holiday. They asked me if I would be willing to donate trucks to deliver the bikes, but I didn't have the resources to pay all the drivers. I decided to ask them if they would be willing to volunteer their time, trucks, and diesel to help. Others in the office said that there was no way our guys would waste their time volunteering. Guess what? Every single driver donated their time to help Houston's kids, and they have continued doing so every year since 2004. These guys are true heroes.

GIVE THEM YOUR FIVE CENTS

How do you show appreciation to your team? If giving positive feedback doesn't come naturally to you, grab a handful of pennies and put them in your right pocket. Make a point of giving positive feedback to your team, and every time you say something positive, move one penny from the right pocket to the left.

You will be surprised at how much a small compliment on a job well done will go in fulfilling an employee's need to be appreciated at work.

I often hear people say that they appreciate someone's work. But is it just the work you appreciate? Instead of saying, "I appreciate you doing that," leave off the last two words. "I appreciate *you*." Being appreciated as a person instead of just the work you produce makes all the hard work worthwhile.

Sometimes you have to give negative feedback. Remember to always give negative feedback in a private setting—never during a meeting or in a group email. Save public settings for positive feedback.

Keeping up with the day-to-day running of your business can be hectic, and you lose sight of the importance of showing your team that you appreciate them. When something is this important, put it on your schedule. Add a reminder on your schedule once a week to remember to send positive notes to your team. I have Thank You Thursdays dedicated to writing a few handwritten notes to my employees and either mailing them or leaving them on their desks so they can be found when they arrive at work in the morning. Emails are easy for people to ignore, so make thank-you cards or even simple Post-it Notes attached to their computer screen. Write specifically what your teammate has done well or what characteristics of their personality you value.

An employee once texted me a picture of a Thank You Thursday card I sent her years ago. She said she was going through a tough time in her life and dug up one of the cards I wrote to her and read it, and it made her feel better. I had completely forgotten writing the card. Small gestures of kindness can go a long way.

As a leader, never underestimate the power of your words. Words matter, especially the words of a leader. Your words can build someone up or scar them for life. It is your choice.

Remember, *people are fragile. Handle with care.*

END OF CHAPTER CHECKLIST

- ❏ Review the Employee's Needs Triangle. Does everyone on your team feel competent, safe, and appreciated?
- ❏ Review the Employee's Needs Triangle with your managers to ensure they understand what your employees need.
- ❏ If you forget to appreciate your employees, try the Five Cents exercise until appreciation becomes natural to you.

END OF PART 3 CHECKLIST

- ❑ I understand the difference between hiring accountable people and holding people accountable.
- ❑ I practice Solo Accountable and make sure only one person is responsible for a task, key indicator, or process.
- ❑ I do not allow managers to blame their direct reports.
- ❑ I am aware of unaccountable language and commit to growing a culture that uses accountable language.
- ❑ I commit to not micromanaging people on my team. I will be OCD when assigning tasks, then I will let my team work with autonomy while still being available if they need help.
- ❑ I evaluate every person on my team using the People Matrix. I create a strategic plan to get rid of any Untouchables or Mascots.
- ❑ I understand why it might be nicer to fire nice people and more profitable for the company to fire top performers.
- ❑ I ask myself, *Which team member would I enthusiastically rehire?*
- ❑ I push back on my direct reports when they come to me to solve their problems. I am a coach, not an answering booth.
- ❑ I understand that it is OK for people to fail, and my people understand that I expect mistakes to happen because mistakes are what lead to innovation.
- ❑ I understand that while motivation is intrinsic, it is possible to demotivate a team.
- ❑ I make sure everyone on my team feels safe, competent, and appreciated.
- ❑ If I am bad at remembering to give positive feedback, I have created a process to ensure that I show my appreciation for my employees' efforts.

PART 4

Do Less to Achieve More

18

Trash Your Business Plan

When we want to know how to get somewhere, most of us use a GPS system, like Google Maps. In order to get where you are going, you need to give the system two data points: where you are now and where you want to go. Then, presto, Google Maps works its magic and gives you a path. This seems pretty simple, yet when we want to lead our people on a path of growth, we often fail to give them these two basic pieces of information. Key indicators can tell our team where they are now, but we need to also communicate where we want to go.

A business plan is the "go-to" document to lead businesses in the right direction. But like many businesses, 3 Men Movers was started by a man who lacked an MBA and was just trying to make enough money to pay the rent and support his family. My dad had no idea how to write a business plan.

While my dad never had a *written* business plan, a vision statement, a mission statement, or core values, he nonetheless *lived* his goals, principles, and values. As he started growing his business, he articulated his values as a mantra that he required his drivers to chant during Monday meetings: "We work hard. We're professional!" At first, the drivers were sheepish and embarrassed, but eventually his idea took hold, and they began to understand his philosophy.

They were much more than blue-collar labor: *Anyone* can move a sofa—*they* were in charge of a crew and were running a business.

The chant raised the men's expectations for themselves. My dad knew that each one of them must believe in their heart that they were entrepreneurs and not just laborers. To this day, we continue to chant—sometimes even shout—this mantra with gusto. He was able to grow his business to $3 million without a business plan because he was able to articulate his vision with everyone on his team.

FROM BUSINESS PLAN TO EXECUTION PLAN

My dad's vision was that 3 Men Movers would one day dominate the Texas Triangle, which is made up of Houston, Dallas–Fort Worth, Austin, and San Antonio, forming a funky triangle on the map. In 2018, the Triangle's economic activity totaled $1.3 trillion, more than the economies of Mexico, Indonesia, or Saudi Arabia.* "We have to get the Triangle," he would say over and over again.

His pursuit of the Triangle became his obsession. Everyone on the team knew that the company's vision was *the Triangle*. He talked about it daily; it was his passion. When he started talking about the Triangle, he would get fired up and wave his hands around wildly.

While he didn't have a written business plan, his ideas for his company were thoroughly thought out and well communicated to everyone on the team. Everyone knew the vision of the company and its values. I know of billion-dollar corporations run by Ivy League CEOs who spent fortunes on fancy retreats and consultants to create mission statements, core values, and vision statements, yet most people in their company have no idea what they are. My dad, on the other hand, had no business degree, but he had strong, effective business instincts. Everyone on his team knew the values and the mission of the company. We were going to conquer the Texas Triangle come hell or high water!

A formal business plan is usually more than thirty pages in length. Some of the standard items included in the business plan are an executive summary, financial projections, analysis of your competitors, size of the marketplace,

---

* Chris Tomlinson, "Tomlinson: Texas Triangle is key to economic growth, but brings big changes," *Houston Chronicle*, November 1, 2021, https://www.houstonchronicle.com/business/columnists/tomlinson/article/texas-triangle-economy-growth-key-big-changes-16570191.php.

information about your industry, and your goals and vision for the company. If you are pursuing investment capital for a start-up, the bank and investors will want to see a detailed business plan. You can create one by finding a template on the Internet, doing your research, and filling it in. The outcome for you will be less about the final product (except for the fact that the bank or investors usually require one) and more about the research involved in creating the business plan.

Researching and writing a formal business plan is a great way to learn about your industry. Taking the time to think about your market and competitors critically is worth the effort if you are going to get involved in a new industry.

What happens next to this long and extensively researched business plan? After it is given to an investor or a banker, it sits on a shelf to collect dust. Even though the process yielded some beneficial insights for you, that beautiful, analytical piece of masterful business writing is still a pretty boring document that nobody but your banker probably cares to read—and only because your banker gets paid for doing so.

Your team needs to understand the direction of the company, and a long business plan is too boring and cumbersome for your team to rally around and get excited about. Instead, a one-page Execution Plan is all you need to give guidance to your team about the direction of your company. An Execution Plan highlights the goals for the company's future in a way that is easy for your team to understand and remember. It should be created yearly with your leadership team, if you have one. If you are a solopreneur, then create one just for your own benefit. Your Execution Plan should contain the following items:

1. A vision statement written in the present tense for a date five years down the road.
2. Your mission statement.
3. A list of your company's core values.
4. Revenue goals and/or standard quality metrics.
5. Your goals for the current year (three to five goals; less is more).
6. Your ninety-day sprints, which are quarterly goals that help you reach your yearly goals. These are measurable or definitive and ensure Solo Accountable ownership from people on your team responsible for achieving the goal.
7. Any other piece of information that you consider crucial for your company that you want to keep in the forefront of your team's mind.

Remember that one page is not a lot of space, so use this real estate wisely for the most important aspects of your Execution Plan. Keep in mind that the above items are suggestions. You should tweak your Execution Plan to meet your company's goals and needs. Gino Wickman offers a good example of how an Execution Plan should look in his book *Traction*. Every business should have a process for organizing and tracking their goals and a formal execution process. Wickman's book is by far the best book I have read on how to organize and execute a company's goals. His Execution Plan is called a VTO, a Vision Traction Organizer.

The Execution Plan should be updated quarterly for your ninety-day sprints and once a year for your yearly goals. A suitable time to work on yearly goal planning would be prior to the start of the next fiscal year. Schedule a yearly strategy session with your team at the beginning of December so that you are ready to hit the ground running with a solidly written Execution Plan on January 1.

When you are setting your vision, don't make the mistake I made. In 2007, our vision statement was that we were going to open in the four major markets in Texas (following my dad's Texas Triangle dream): "3 Men Movers is a trusted household name and the largest moving company in Houston, Dallas–Fort Worth, San Antonio, and Austin." It sounded like a great vision statement.

But for three straight years, we made zero progress toward fulfilling the vision. I had made an amateur mistake and didn't assign a date for when we would achieve this goal. There was no deadline; therefore, there was no sense of urgency. When I updated the vision statement with a date, we achieved our goal a year ahead of schedule.

YOU ARE THE TOP SALESPERSON

As the owner of your company, you are in sales. As a matter of fact, you are the top salesperson in your company! Your job is to sell your vision to your team. If you fail at getting buy-in from your team, you won't reach your company's goals.

Unlike a business plan, an Execution Plan is written for your team, not your bank or investors. Everyone should be on the same page. The people on your team are your customers, the Execution Plan is your marketing collateral for "selling" your vision, and you are the lead salesperson. It is one of the most important pieces of marketing collateral within your company.

Now this is where the important part comes into play. Take your one-page plan, add your company logo, and make it colorful and graphically stunning. If you have a Marketing department, ask them to format it so that it "pops." Review the words you use and tweak them to be more of a marketing piece. Keep everything positive. Rewrite the goals so they are appealing and motivating. To move forward, you want everyone rowing together, and the Execution Plan is crucial for showing everyone which direction they should be rowing.

Next, make it visible to the entire team. Have a company-wide meeting each quarter when you publish your updated Execution Plan. During that presentation, take time to go over the previous quarter's wins and losses, review your plan for the next quarter, and discuss how things look for the year. If you have strong department managers within your organization, let them gain experience by presenting all or part of the next ninety-day sprints so they improve their speaking and leadership skills. Place copies in the lunchroom, on the backs of the bathroom doors, and on bulletin boards. Send it to the graphics person and have it printed in large format to post on the wall. Sing it from the rooftop and get everyone involved. Don't stop until even the janitor knows what the Execution Plan is and how he as an individual can contribute to his company's vision.

> **Your Execution Plan is the most important marketing piece. It markets your vision to your team!**

If everyone knows the plan, they can all pull together as a team to accomplish it. Again, people want to have some sort of purpose in their work. Often, owners of small companies create goals and share them with their spouses but never share their complete vision with their work team. If you store your vision in your head, then you end up working toward it alone. If nobody on your team knows the destination—where the company wants to be in three or five years—then they are much less likely to help the company move in the right direction.

Sharing your long-term goals with your team will give them a deeper understanding of how their daily tasks fit into the big picture of helping the company achieve its big goals. Carrying the entire burden of the company's vision on your own will make work much harder and more stressful. By sharing this burden of responsibility, you will also share the joy of reaching these goals, sometimes the disappointment of defeat, and all the struggles in between. You will ignite your team and create excitement around a common, shared goal.

An engaged team is a force multiplier.

Remember, communicating your Execution Plan both visually and vocally will help engage your team.

Although a long, well-written business plan has its place, which is more effective in igniting a team? The one-page Execution Plan is visible and easy for your team to read and understand. Documenting goals keeps your team accountable. If you also use a verbal mantra to reinforce your vision and values like my dad did, you will have the best of both worlds.

END OF CHAPTER REVIEW

Create a one-page Execution Plan. Use this template as an example:

COMPANY LOGO	Vision Statement:	
	Mission Statement:	
Core Values:	Revenue Goal:	Profit Goal:
	Yearly Goals:	
90-DAY SPRINT QUARTER 1			
Owner	Commitment	Date:

END OF CHAPTER CHECKLIST

- ❑ Create an Execution Plan and ensure it has the following:
  - Vision statement, where your company will be in three to five years.
  - Mission statement: your *Why*.
  - Core values: What your company stands for.
  - Your company's logo and colors: Make it a marketing piece.
  - Current year's revenue and profit goals.
  - Current year's measurable goals (three to five).
  - First quarter goals.
- ❑ Set a date to announce your Execution Plan to the team.
- ❑ Distribute by printing, emailing, and posting so that everyone understands the direction in which the company is going.
- ❑ Incorporate the Execution Plan during meetings and 1-2-1s to ensure the activities are aligned with the goals.
- ❑ Create monthly benchmarks to ensure you are on track to reach your yearly goals.

19

Build a Culture That Repels

Every company has values, whether you take the time to print them and stick them on your wall or not. Sometimes a company's real values don't match the written values. Take a look at the following core values.

1. **Communication:** We have an obligation to communicate.
2. **Respect:** We treat others as we would like to be treated.
3. **Integrity:** We work with customers and prospects openly, honestly, and sincerely.
4. **Excellence:** We are satisfied with nothing less than the best in everything we do.

Sounds good, right?

These are the core values that were listed in Enron's annual report to shareholders. Obviously, the written statement didn't match the actual values of the leadership team. Instead of *integrity*, their corrupt business practices, which were certainly not made public and most certainly not *communicated*, eventually destroyed the company and their employees' savings, thus devastating thousands of people's lives. They certainly failed on values 1–3, and as for 4, unless they were trying to achieve *excellence* by robbing people, they failed on that one too. Enron's true values were not *respectful* to their shareholders and employees. Their real value was greed, by creating profits by any means necessary, regardless of ethics.

Values within an organization tend to reflect the values of a company's leader. I heard a story from my business mentor about a man he was mentoring. This man's company displayed its core values written in the lobby, but his personal values were not aligned with the fancy mural in his waiting area. The business owner was a dishonest person and was always trying to pull one over on his customers and employees. He would add frivolous expenses to customers' bills to milk them for a bit more money. He would cut benefits and scheme ways to lower his payroll costs. He was trying to squeeze a little more out of each situation without creating more value. He was an all-around dirtbag.

Good people within his company, when faced with his corrupt business practices, would leave. Good people wouldn't put up with his treatment of his customers or his staff. After a while, his company consisted of people who accepted his crooked behavior, people just like him.

My mentor had the unique quality of always being able to see good in everyone. He worked hard to help this businessman see his flaws and improve. One day the business owner came to my mentor and told him about a person in his accounting office who embezzled money from the company. The owner was upset and shocked. My mentor used this story as a lesson. This businessman had created a culture of unethical behavior based on his core values. The honest people within his company had departed, and he was left with people who shared his core values. These were employees who were OK with him pulling one over on someone—and that someone in this instance ended up being the business owner himself.

CREATE A CULTURE THAT REPELS

Companies that hire and fire on values tend to have magnetic cultures. Magnets attract people who fit in and repel people who don't. Your culture should be intensely strong to the point of being extremely attractive to the right candidates. Often, we forget that a magnet has two sides. Your company should also work like the opposite side of a magnet and repel people who don't fit.

One of the strongest core values at our company is our work ethic, based originally on my dad's work ethic and discipline. Occasionally we make a bad hire, and after the honeymoon phase of the first few months, we notice that an employee does not fit our hardworking culture. We might see the employee taking extended breaks, not finishing work assignments, or surfing the web for extended periods of time.

When someone doesn't fit our hardworking culture, the entire team turns against this person and wants them gone quickly. If hard work is one of your core values, then the more you get rid of people who don't fit and hire those who do fit, the stronger the company's values become. Pretty soon you will have a homogeneous culture of hard workers.

This is also true with leadership. Once I hired one of the most intelligent people I have ever met to run a department at 3 Men Movers, but he didn't have our core value of respect. He would patronize people who could not keep up with his intellect. Even his compliments were given with a condescending smile.

I discussed the Employee's Needs Triangle, though it had no effect with him. This manager made the employees feel incompetent, and the team set about to take this guy out: It became *Mutiny on the Bounty*. They went around him to another manager when they needed help because the other manager didn't make them feel stupid when they had a question.

People choose their leaders, and at times it isn't the person you assigned to lead them. Some people who worked directly for this person were instantly repelled and quit their job. We began to lose more good people. Eventually, we had to let him go. While this person was phenomenally intelligent and capable, my team held the value of respect in higher importance than intelligence.

FIRING CUSTOMERS

We expect our employees to treat one another with respect. We also require respect from our customers, or we will fire our customers. Our contractors have full authority to leave a customer's house if they are not being treated with respect.

Once, we had a customer who was saying horrible, racist things to one of our movers. The mover called me, and I could hear the customer yelling in the background. I was so proud of our guy for having the fortitude to not react in an unprofessional way to the customer. He said, "Sir, I am trying to help you. If you continue to talk to me this way, I am going to leave." When the customer continued his rant, the mover packed up his equipment and walked off the job. I was fully supportive of his decision, even though we lost money on the job.

When your core values are important, it is worth losing money to honor them. We will always put our people over profits. While it is understandable that moving is stressful and customers can get upset, there is a boundary that we will not allow our customers to cross. Never allow a member of your work team to be treated disrespectfully.

IF THE SHOE DOESN'T FIT

Values change when new leadership takes over. My dad could be temperamental, and while he had a big heart, he liked to yell, or at least he thought he needed to be in fight mode to run a business. During the last few years of his life, when he could finally relax, he became super mellow and sweet. I think that was who he always was at his core. While he was running the company, the thought that he might fail so consumed him with dread that it governed his behavior and put him in fight mode.

When I took over, I tried to lead the company the way he did, thinking that this was how you rule when you become the boss. I tried to walk in his shoes, but his shoes were not comfortable for me. I was not a heavy-handed, autocratic leader. I wanted to be tough like him because I associated his leadership style with strength. I figured that it was a sign of weakness that I didn't want to get in people's faces.

With time, I became comfortable with my unique leadership style. While I have strong boundaries, I value calmness and peace. I have created a culture in which people can work and not hear any voices raised in anger.

I once let a manager go for slamming a door hard when he was angry. There were other events that led up to this, but this act of aggression was the final straw. Slamming doors didn't fit our culture. Everyone has their own style of leadership, and your employees will self-select based on whether it is a style they can embrace and either stay with you or choose to leave.

You can gauge your culture by conducting a company survey and asking your employees to describe their culture. We recently won best-places-to-work awards, and one of the award companies sent us a word-cloud made up of the most repeated words our employees offered when asked how they would describe their job. The words repeated from employees on the front line are much more indicative of your company's culture than what executives come up with in a corporate retreat. What words would your frontline employees choose for your company? *Stressful, disorganized, boring*? Or *challenging, rewarding, fun*? What word-cloud would your employees create?

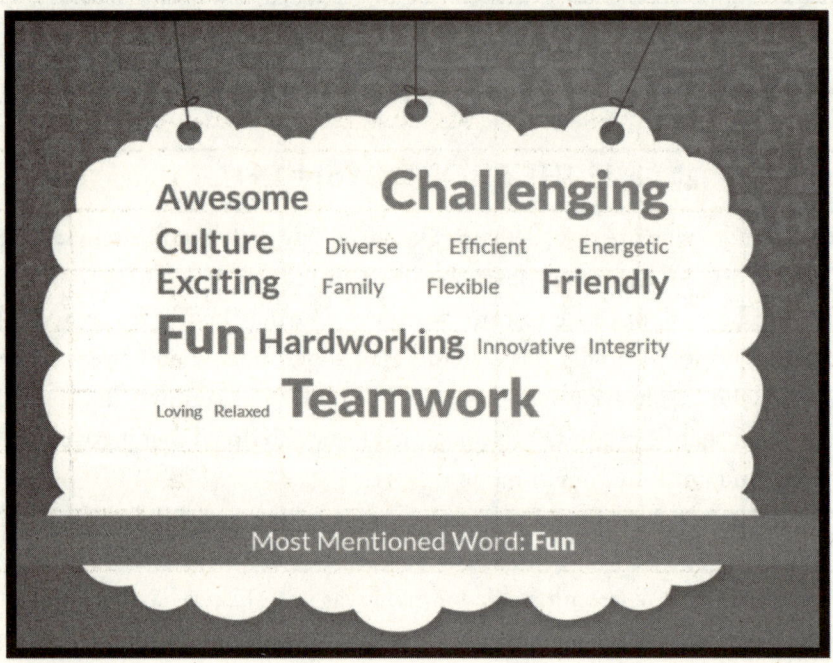

END OF CHAPTER CHECKLIST

- ☐ List the core values in your company.
- ☐ Grade your employees on whether their behavior reflects the company's core values. If you have a leadership team, have them grade the employees too. Do a "blind" grading so nobody will be influenced by others' grades.
- ☐ Do core value grading quarterly, and notice if a person is lacking your core values over multiple quarters. It is a huge red flag that your company is complacent with who you allow on your team, and not getting bad fits off the team. This can potentially erode your culture.
- ☐ If you have no feedback, good or bad, give the employee a 0. If the employee sometimes lacks your core values, give them a 1. If they often

lack your core values, give them a 2. If they never display your company's core values, give them a 3.

Example (you will have different values so your chart will look different):

CORE VALUE GRADING					
	Respect	Teamwork	High Work Ethic	Positive Attitude	TOTAL
Tracy	0	0	0	1	1
Morgan	1	0	0	1	2
Kevin	2	3	2	2	9
Justin	0	0	0	0	0
Chris	0	1	0	1	2
Anna	0	0	1	2	3
TOTAL	3	4	3	7	

Notice in the bottom row how the overall company's score is high for having a negative attitude.

When you see a high score throughout your entire team on a particular value, then that isn't a true company value at the time the grade was given. This indicates that you need to work on changing your culture or changing your written values. Maybe your value is "Fun" and instead your team is more "Focused." You have a choice between changing the company's value from Fun to Focused, or trying to create goals around having more fun in the office.

On the last column to the right, you can see the individual scores. It looks like Kevin isn't a good fit for your company. If you hire and fire based on core values, Kevin's days should be numbered.

20
It's Not About You

> We are what we repeatedly do.
> Excellence, then, is not an act, but a habit.
> **—Will Durant**

Companies thrive on discipline and process. When I was twenty-nine and started running a business, those two words—*discipline* and *process*—did not describe me. I was an artsy young woman, and running on set schedules wasn't in my nature. It felt stifling. However, I found that, as I became more organized, the company ran better and my employees felt more content. Companies, like people, like routines.

THE MEETING WAS ABOUT ME

As I said, my early meetings were a mess. I would pick a random date and notify my team that we were going to have a meeting. Sometimes, when I was feeling more disciplined, I would keep a weekly meeting schedule, but it was always on a different day of the week and at a different time of the day. Most often, we would fall out of doing weekly meetings. Then, when things would come to a head and we needed some extra communication, I would send out an email with a meeting time, and we would decide to meet as a team. There was no regularly scheduled meeting where my team could get updates, ask questions, and collaborate on solving problems.

If something came up in my schedule, I would be late or postpone the meeting for another random date in the future. When we did have meetings, my poor team members would be sitting around the table patiently waiting for me, and I would arrive ten to fifteen minutes late while apologizing with some "good" excuse.

Nobody was expected to show up prepared with anything, except me. I would have my talking points that I would pull out and go over. These were things that I thought they needed to know, mostly housekeeping. I would do most of the talking unless I had a question, and then someone would speak up in response. I would then delegate work to each person, and the meeting would end. The work that was delegated might or might not be followed up on in the future, depending on if I remembered. Sometimes I had a scheduling conflict, and I would have to leave the meeting early. When this happened, the entire meeting would come to a halt.

I can see now that the meetings back then were 100 percent about me. I arranged the meetings. I set the agenda. I prepared. I did the talking. The meeting started when I walked into the room and ended when I walked out of the room. My team was completely disengaged.

Company meetings should be about the company.

Even if you purposely avoid an asshole organizational structure, and you push back and empower your people so that you are not at the center of every decision, if you are running your meetings like I was when I started, *you are still the company asshole!* The company is revolving around the boss instead of on the company's vision and mission.

THE LEADERSHIP TEAM MEETING

In 2010, I decided that I'd had enough of our boring meetings. I had recently taken a class at Rice where I learned that all meetings should have a set agenda: *No agenda, no attenda*. I know some of you reading this probably know this is an obvious rule. I didn't. I decided to create a process for the weekly meetings and delegate it to someone other than me, which would allow me to skip meetings as needed. I created an agenda, printed it out, and set a regular meeting date for Mondays at 9:30 AM. I told my team to start the meetings without me regardless of whether I was late. And eventually they did.

But it didn't happen all at once. At first, when I would arrive late, my team members would be hanging out, chatting, and politely waiting for me, but after I reminded them that at ten minutes past the scheduled start of the meeting they should be at a certain part of the agenda that was written and laid out in front of them, they started to get the hang of it. Little did I know that process I put in place because I wanted to play hooky from the weekly meetings ended up being the game changer my company needed to create rapid growth. This was the start of the meetings being about the company and not about me.

In time, my team took complete control of the leadership team meetings. The leadership team became fully engaged. They had to be; they were running the show now. They followed a set agenda, brought issues to the table to discuss, and created OCDs for tasks that needed to be done. Instead of listening to me talking for 90 percent of the time, *they* were fully participating. Then a funny thing happened.

I went from dreading attending the weekly meetings to showing up on time to every one of them. I didn't want to miss out on what was going on in the company. Nobody likes to miss out on important information that they need to do their job. Nobody likes to get left behind. When I was doing all the talking, I wasn't listening. Now I could hear what was happening from their point of view. Now I was learning. My company was moving forward with or without me. I wanted to be a part of it. What started as a sneaky way for me to be able to skip boring meetings ended up being a catalyst for being on time and becoming fully engaged in every meeting.

Now we have a set agenda, and my team runs the weekly meetings. We run the meetings based on the EOS method from Gino Wickman's book *Traction*. We modified it a bit to fit our needs within our industry.

The team comes prepared for meetings. They show up with their department's key indicators, issues they need help with, and news they want to share. During the entire process, we are creating action items and using the OCD method. Our deadline is always on the day of the meetings so we can check off completed tasks at each weekly meeting.

Once we made the meetings *about the company*, things really began to change. My department managers took more ownership of their work. They began to run their departments as though they were owners of micro-companies within our company. They were reporting to each other and not to me, and I was no longer the center of the organizational structure. I wasn't *that asshole*, because instead of my team focusing on me, I replaced myself with our vision and goals. When I was able to pull myself out of the middle of everything and be a part of the team, I was able to work *with* them toward a common goal instead of working *on* them, pushing them to reach the goal.

They began pushing themselves. They challenged each other. They didn't use or accept unaccountable language. They asked each other, "Is this an action item?" when an idea was presented, and if it was an action item, they documented it with OCD. I got to sit back and watch the magic.

> **You never know what people are capable of until you give them the opportunity.**

When I look at the differences between lower-performing companies and 3 Men Movers, the biggest difference is my people and their capacity to accomplish our shared goals. Other business owners ask me how I find such amazing people. I agree that my people are exceptional, but chances are they have some exceptional people on their team—unfortunately, they are being handcuffed.

My people have been given the opportunity to work independently. Yes, we have processes that we follow, but within these processes, they are able to run their departments as they see fit. They understand the vision and what their team is accountable for. The biggest difference between my teams and others' is that I step out of their way.

BEFORE:

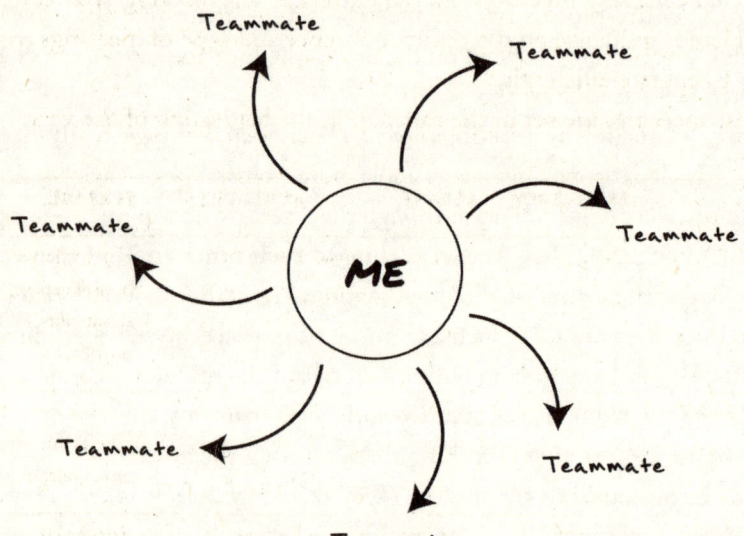

AFTER:

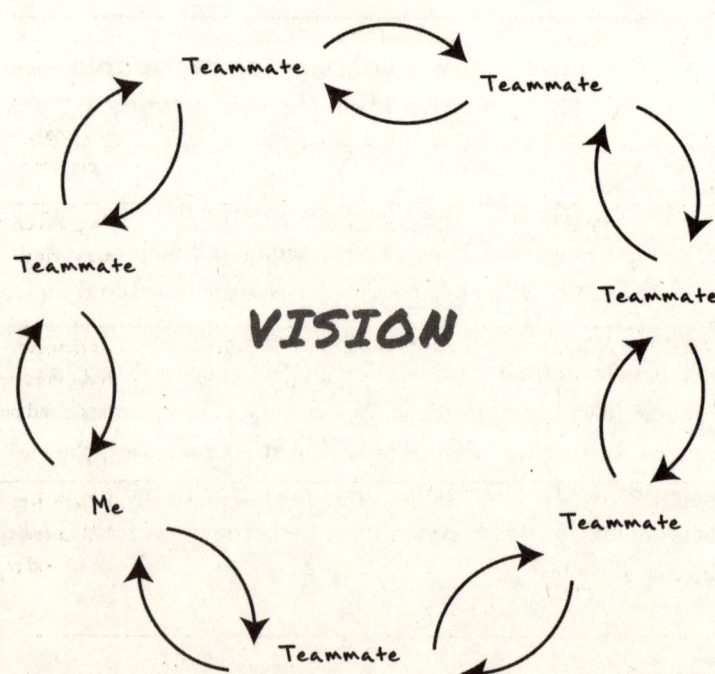

OPTIMIZE YOUR COMPANY MEETINGS

Disciplined company meetings are the pathways to executing your company's vision. Here is guidance on the optimal number and type of meetings required in order to operate efficiently.

These meetings are set in the calendar at the beginning of the year.

TYPE	FREQUENCY	LENGTH	ATTENDEES	PURPOSE
HUDDLE	Daily	5 minutes or less	Entire staff	Key Indicators, housekeeping, shout-outs, all positive.
QUARTERLY	Quarterly	4–6 hours	Management	Review last quarter sprints and create next quarter sprints.
COMPANY-WIDE	Quarterly	20 minutes	Entire staff	Review last quarter sprints and announce next quarter sprints.
YEARLY	Yearly	1–2 days	Management	Review last year's goals, create next year's goals, and grade team members.
1-2-1s/1-2-2s	Weekly	30–60 minutes	1 or 2 Direct Reports/Manager	Progress check and mentoring.
LEADERSHIP	Weekly	60–90 minutes	Management	Review Key Indicators, sprints, tasks, and problem solve.
DEPARTMENT	Weekly	60 minutes	Management	Review Key Indicators, sprints, tasks, and problem solve.

Your managers are the hub between the leadership team and the rest of the staff. Crucial information must be communicated from the leadership team meetings to the rest of the staff, and concerns from the staff must be communicated back to the leadership team. The head of the department who attends both meetings is a conduit for the flow of communication in both directions, keeping everyone on the same page.

As a business owner, you have it easy. You only need to meet with your department heads during the weekly leadership meeting and have 1-2-1s with your department heads. You don't have to attend the huddles, but it means a lot to your team to see your face bright and early. I love attending huddles and even do so sometimes when I am on vacation. I'm not checking up on my team—instead, I enjoy having my coffee for five to ten minutes with my coworkers, which is an enjoyable way to start my day.

I am committed to my weekly meeting schedule and have that time blocked off and dedicated to my team. My leadership meeting runs ninety minutes, and I have five department heads whom I meet with for a one-hour 1-2-1 weekly. Altogether I am in meetings for about six-and-a-half hours a week, and the effort has paid off.

The following are samples of specific meetings.

Yearly Strategy Meeting

When: Once a year before January 1, or before your fiscal year starts.
Duration: Anywhere from one to two days depending on the team-building events scheduled.
Who Attends: Department heads and/or key employees.
Objective: A yearly strategy meeting is a chance to review last year's financials, key indicators, and goals. It is also an opportunity to discuss what is working and what isn't, brainstorm ideas, and process issues. Your team will create first-quarter ninety-day sprints. The final objective is to set yearly goals with benchmarks and create an Execution Plan for the next year that can be shared company wide.

A yearly strategy session usually lasts one or two full days. If possible, have this meeting off-site so your team is not interrupted by day-to-day work issues. Getting away from your business's hubbub of daily activities will allow your team to focus. You can rent out a small conference room in a hotel, or if you have business friends, ask them if you can borrow an unused conference room. My bank allows me to use their meeting spaces for free.

If you can afford to hire a business coach to facilitate the meeting, do so. If you're not running the meeting yourself, you can get out of the center of everything and instead of leading the meeting you can be a participant in the meeting. This allows you to be less of an administrator and more of a strategist. But if you don't have the resources for this approach, that's OK: The most important thing is that you are coming together to create written goals that you will share with the rest of the company. Part of this meeting should be a free flow of ideas where everyone brainstorms about the future vision of the company. This will be the only time you don't have to be OCD.

QUARTERLY MEETINGS

When: At the end of each quarter.
Duration: Leadership should usually take half a day; departments can extend their regularly scheduled weekly meetings by an hour.
Who Attends: The entire leadership team, and for the department sprint meeting, the entire department.
Objective: During a quarterly meeting, you will review the last ninety-day sprints and set new ones for the next quarter. You will also review the yearly goals to see if you are making progress toward achieving them. Some companies will review financials and grade employees on whether they are a cultural fit.

Ninety-day sprints are held every quarter. They should be held at a leadership level and at a departmental level. It is better, but not mandatory, to hold the leadership meetings off-site. Remember to plan a celebration every ninety days, either at a company level or a department level, to celebrate big wins when you succeed in your ninety-day sprint goals.

WEEKLY LEADERSHIP AND DEPARTMENT MEETINGS

When: Every week.
Duration: Sixty to ninety minutes.
Who Attends: All department heads for the leadership team meeting and the entire department for the weekly department meeting.

Objective: Weekly meetings are held not only to achieve your yearly goals and ninety-day sprints but also to get through issues that come up in the day-to-day activities while you work. As companies move away from the start-up phase, the weekly meetings are an integral part of fostering communication between teams.

Weekly meetings should be held for both the leadership team and with each department. During this time, the group should go over key indicators, solve problems, and delegate work.

My teams start off the leadership meeting with a check-in that includes updates of anything they want to share about their personal lives. Maybe they talk about a party they went to, a movie they recently saw, or an accomplishment they achieved. Sometimes there is sad news: a parent diagnosed with cancer, a death of a family member or pet. The check-in is a chance for everyone on your team to know where their teammates are personally and, if needed, a way to understand if someone on your team will need a little extra support in their lives.

Make sure your team isn't overpromising what they can finish by the next weekly meeting date. One talented and ambitious recent college graduate promised to have every task assigned to him completed by Monday, yet each Monday we would go over what he accomplished, and he always fell short. It wasn't because of his lack of effort or talent, but because, in his eagerness to prove himself and please the group, he overcommitted. Remember, say = do* (*always). He needed to say less. He was overcommitting.

After a few embarrassing check-ins during which he had to tell the group he was unable to finish his work, he learned quickly not to overcommit. Now, he pushes back and says that his current workload will not allow him the time to finish this new task until the following week. I am proud of him for taking control of his time management and knowing when to push back on a deadline. When a person on your team member tells you "No," it shows that they trust you enough to be honest if something can't be done. It is much better to hear a "No" now than "I didn't finish" when the project was scheduled to be completed.

On occasion, I might feel the new task is more important than his current projects. In these cases, I let him know so he can shuffle some things around, but normally I allow him to be accountable for his due dates. It is our job to make our team feel safe enough to tell us when they feel like something can't be achieved.

If you force due dates on your team and they don't complete their work, whose fault is it when the task doesn't get completed? You don't know exactly what is on their plate. Allowing your team to control their workload and choose their own deadlines increases their level of personal accountability. To allow them to own their project, ask them, "When do you think you can have that done?" When they give you a date, ask, "Are you sure? Because if you need more time, tell me. Whatever date you commit to I will expect you to honor and have your task complete."

1-2-1 MEETINGS

When: Once a week.
Duration: Forty-five minutes.
Who Attends: Lead and one or two direct reports.
Objective: 1-2-1s are an opportunity to check in and ensure the people you manage have the feedback and resources they need to complete their ninety-day sprints and daily tasks. It is a time to process issues that are affecting their performance.

Every employee should have a weekly 1-2-1 or 1-2-2 with their manager weekly. 1-2-1s should last approximately forty-five minutes. These meetings should be seen as a weekly fixture in your manager's schedule. The best way to ensure this gets into your schedule is to block off a morning or two and make it reoccur in your calendar. My 1-2-1s are in the mornings from Monday to Wednesday. If a business colleague or vendor wants to meet with me during these times I don't even have to look at my calendar because I know this time is always booked. This time is a sacred time that I share with my direct reports, and except for a vacation or an illness, they happen like clockwork. 1-2-1s, like all meetings, should start and end on time.

Note: A manager of a big department might have difficulty meeting with each person on their team weekly. If this is the case, then they should combine 1-2-1s and instead have 1-2-2s so that they can get through their weekly meetings in half the time. Sometimes the dynamics of a 1-2-2 can be more beneficial because you can meet with a new employee and an older employee at the same time, and they are able to learn from each other. It also develops more camaraderie within your teams. I find that three 1-2-1s are a comfortable number to hold in a day. I usually have four a day and that is pushing it, because you have to maintain your attention for almost four hours. Even Steven Spielberg, with a multimillion-dollar budget, has a hard time making a movie that will keep you focused for four hours. I would recommend against having more than four 1-2-1s. Doing so will have you so drained that you will be unable to give your last employee the energy and focus they deserve.

Your direct reports should be 100 percent responsible for managing their 1-2-1s. They should arrive with a list of topics they want to discuss. You should not have to chase them down for this meeting. It is their responsibility to show up on time. This is their time, and you should mentor them on things *they* want to talk about. They should be doing 80 percent of the talking. If the manager shows up with the agenda, takes control of the meetings, does all the talking, then the manager is doing it wrong.

You will notice that over time your direct reports will start gathering things they want to talk about in advance of their 1-2-1s. This will lower your stress level during the week because they won't be at your office door a few times a day whenever things come up. Instead, they will note it and bring up an issue during their 1-2-1.

Often, managers complain that 1-2-1s take too long. "I don't have time!" A manager's number one job is to lead people. These meetings are part of their job. If a manager oversees six people, and they have a question or two for their manager each day, then the manager is being interrupted every hour. If they have a formally schedule 1-2-1 each week, many of the interruptions can be solved during their 1-2-1s, thus allowing managers to have more uninterrupted work time during the week.

1-2-1s can actually be time savers. Encourage your managers to push back when they are being interrupted for low-priority questions during the week that can wait until a 1-2-1. "I don't mind helping you, but can this wait until our 1-2-1, or is this urgent?"

Yearly reviews are filled with anxiety for both the employee and for management. Management is supposed to communicate progress; however, they tend to give a watered-down version of how an employee is really doing. Here is an example of what should happen and what actually happens during a review with a scoring system of 1–5.

What Happens
5 Good
4 Not so Good
3 Bad
2 Don't let the door hit you on the way out.
1 (Never used)

What Should Happen
5 Excels
4 Good
3 Average
2 Not so Good
1 Bad

A 5 ends up meaning *normal*, and 3 means *needs improvement*, when in reality 5 should mean *above and beyond*, and 3 should mean *meets expectations*. The inflation occurs because a leader waits all year to speak to someone about their performance, and then they feel uncomfortable to give their direct report anything below a 3.

Why wait once a year to communicate with an employee? Between the 1-2-1s and MBWA (Management by Walking Around), people on your team should know, at all times, how they are performing. MBWA is crucial for successful communication. The days when managers hid in their corner offices working on financial statements and charts are over. As a leader, you should spend the majority of your time meeting with your key people and, if time permits, walking around your plant or business. You should know your people so well that when someone on your team walks in the door and says, "Hi," you know immediately by the look on their face and the tone of their voice if something is wrong.

Think like a football coach whose team's performance is based on how it does on the field: Your company's success hinges on the success of your team's performance while working. The coach of a football team doesn't sit in the coach's office; he is in the locker room and on the field. How else can the coach improve their performance? Does he sit in his office and read a report about what they did all day? Does he wait for another player to come in and say, "John hasn't been making interceptions today"? No, he is down on the field watching performance firsthand.

Today we are bombarded with emails, reports, and the need to document and analyze numbers. All of these things are important, but nothing is more important than getting into the trenches and engaging with your team. There is nothing I get more return on investment from than spending an hour each week in 1-2-1s with each one of my direct reports.

THE MORNING HUDDLE MEETING

When: Every morning.
Duration: Five minutes maximum.
Who Attends: Everyone.
Objective: The daily huddle is a "Rah rah, let's slay the day" meeting sprinkled with some housekeeping and a few metrics. The goal is to get everyone on the same page.

The morning huddle should last a maximum of five minutes but more likely runs no more than two to three minutes. The huddle should be 99 percent positive because this is the meeting that will set the tone of the day for your team. The meeting should be upbeat and brisk. If the meeting becomes synonymous with negative feedback, then nobody will look forward to it. Clearly state your progress toward your goals by reviewing key indicators from the day before or month to date. Read some great reviews. Say some happy birthdays. Let the team know if something is going on in the facility—for example, the front printer is broken, or the repair person will arrive between ten and eleven. Give some shout-outs—for example, to Norma for being such a team player and staying late the previous night. Then adjourn. That's it!

Make sure that different people run the meeting, and make sure that person isn't *you*! Remember, everything should be about the company, and the vision and your meeting time isn't an opportunity for you to climb onto your daily soapbox.

3 Men Movers has been growing at a rate of over four times our industry average consistently for the last twenty years, and it isn't due to some new great idea or random chance, either. It requires discipline. Our disciplined meeting structure is integral to our success.

Remote work changes things, but not as much as you might think. During COVID, my employees went home for safety reasons, and they wanted to have a hybrid policy when it was time to come back to the office. Every meeting in this chapter can be done remotely. Our daily huddle became crucial to make human connections, and with a push from the employees we started the huddle five minutes early for anyone who wanted to join. I thought, *Who is going to want to log in five minutes earlier in the morning?* The answer: almost everyone! The team wanted socialization time, and now, for the first five minutes, we log on and just socialize. The early five-minute check-in isn't mandatory, yet almost everyone checks in to chat with their peers and drink coffee together. Work isn't just about work; it is about community, and even with remote work, you have to make an effort to build community.

PINEAPPLE PIZZA

Sometimes the strangest things bring people together. With my team, it is picking a side on whether pineapple is an appropriate topping on a pizza. There is a constant heated battle about it, all in good fun. When a new employee starts, we quickly figure out what side they are on during the pre-huddle meeting. Lots of laughter and smack talking ensues.

We realize that we are a tribe of humans, and now our tribe is broken up across the United States, with some people in other countries. We have to make an extra effort to make a connection with people.

Some of the ways we connect remotely are the following.

- **Meetings:** We still have all the meetings we did in the office. The huddle is our most important meeting now, as it sets the tone for the day and allows everyone to connect first thing in the morning as a team.
- **Lounges:** We created a chat lounge where people can virtually meet up by logging into a video call during breaks, with or without their camera, to just chat with a coworker.
- **Clubs:** We have set up club chats for people who share the same interests. We have a gardening club, a cooking club, a music club, a TV show discussion club, and a business club. You participate only in clubs that interest you. As a company we voted on which clubs we wanted to set up. We share recipes, discuss the new *Game of Thrones* series, share pictures of our tomatoes. These clubs are a way to find common ground and make meaningful connections.

- **Celebrations and Games:** We also have birthday parties and games through video calls. We have silly games like, Are You Smarter Than a First Grader?, or Dad Trivia Night for Father's Day. These represent another way to form a cohesive community with your peers when you can't be in the same room.
- **Memes, GIFs, and Emojis:** Years ago, I would say there was absolutely no place in a professional workplace for this "goofy stuff." Now it is common. Using chat is one dimensional and devoid of emotions. These tools are just another form of communication between my staff and are used to understand content.

    For Example: In the cooking club, one might post the following.

    Annalisa: I had pineapple pizza last night!
    Norma: That sounds great 🙂
    JJ: Yeah, amazing 🤢

    I have been converted. As crazy as it seems, it is all about building a community. I used to say if I don't hear laughter during the day on my floor, I am worried about my culture. Now, if I don't see some good GIFs and emojis, I am worried.

END OF CHAPTER CHECKLIST

Ensure that all your company meetings have the following characteristics:

- ❑ Set a specific day of the week and time of the day. If it is randomly set, it can get randomly canceled. Set your meetings in stone, then work your schedule around your meetings.
- ❑ Hold all group meetings (leadership team meetings and department meetings) on time regardless of whether a key person or even the owner or a department manager is in attendance. *The meeting is greater than any one individual team member, even the owner.* The reason for the meeting is to discuss the tasks that need to be accomplished to reach the company's vision.
- ❑ Create a written agenda with times next to each segment for all group meetings and 1-2-1s, and include a list of all meeting attendees.

- ❏ Start with a check-in process to check the temperature of people on your team. Basically, they can share what they feel comfortable sharing. If it is a larger group, limit it to "Share the biggest one thing that has happened to you since we last met." Doing so will narrow down their answers and speed things up.
- ❏ Choose a person to run the meeting. This person's job is to monitor the time and document action items. People can and should take turns in this role.
- ❏ Monitor key indicators to determine if people within the team or department are performing according to expectations.
- ❏ Check in on individual, department, and company yearly goals and ninety-day sprints.
- ❏ Bring up problems that need to be resolved.
- ❏ Review delegated weekly tasks to ensure that the tasks are being completed on time.
- ❏ Encourage your employees to push back on deadline dates if they think they are unreasonable.
- ❏ Grade the meeting at the end.

21

Ideas Kill

Throughout my childhood, on January 1, my dad asked me to list my New Year's resolutions for the upcoming year. These resolutions revolved around childish pursuits like getting certain grades, starting to paint, or riding my bike. When I began working at 3 Men Movers, I added the company's yearly goals to my personal New Year's resolutions. I have created yearly company goals since 2005, and when I look back at them, I have noticed that every year they are more strategic and better thought-out. There is a reason my strategy improved, and I can't take credit for it.

When I started out, I sat down between Christmas and New Year's and wrote the company goals by myself. I didn't get any input from my team, and I didn't share the written final product with them afterward. Nobody knew the goals except me. After a few years, I began "unveiling" them to our team to make sure we were all on the same page. *My page!*

Remember how we discussed how to find a specific location using Google Maps? To generate directions, you need your current location and the destination location. By not sharing our goals, I was failing to let my team know the destination. If they don't know the destination, they are going to have a hard time figuring out how to get us there. Eventually, I began to invite my leadership team to off-site strategy sessions to create and document the company's goals together.

Now, at the end of each year, we reach out to everyone within our organization for feedback before we start our leadership strategy session. Then, after we meet and review the entire company's input, we create our yearly goals and publish the goals to make them visible for the rest of our organization.

I have found that the more I include my team in the planning, the more success we have in reaching our goals. It seems obvious that having a group of people work toward a goal would be more advantageous than just one person—you—working toward a goal, but I know many business owners who do not include their employees in company goal setting. Involve your team. The goals should be based on the vision of the company and where you want to be five years from now. Each year gets you one step closer to achieving the company's vision.

Now that you have everyone involved, how many goals should you set for the year? My favorite professor, Margaret Cording, who taught strategy, once said the most important decision a leader can make is not which ideas to say "Yes" to, but which ideas to say "No" to.

PLAN LESS, ACCOMPLISH MORE

As an entrepreneur and business owner, you have exciting new ideas hitting you daily. Of course, all of these ideas that come rushing in seem amazing and must be implemented *now*. It takes discipline to refrain from pulling your team off a project to focus on the next million-dollar idea. As a business owner, I realize that *the less we decide to do, the more we can accomplish.*

I joke around that I let my people do whatever they want whenever they want. I say this during speaking engagements to get people to perk up and listen, but it is true. For the most part, the people on my team pick out their yearly goals and their ninety-day sprints. Because they know ahead of time the company's three- to five-year vision, they focus on what their department can do this year to help the company reach its vision. Some audience members ask if letting employees choose their own work is dangerous: If you let people decide what they want to work on, won't they have a tendency to "walk the dog" and set goals that are not challenging enough?

I have found that, if you have a good team, they will push themselves harder than you would ever push them. My job involves looking at their goals and sometimes pulling them back to something that is more achievable. My team thinks they can do way more than they can in the amount of time they are given—they don't aim for a low target; usually their target is too high!

When setting goals, people often think they can conquer the world. In their eagerness to succeed, they may create eight or more goals, which, unless they can delegate to a virtual army of coworkers, would be impossible to accomplish because their focus would be spread too thin. If they have eight goals on their list, ask them to look over what they want to do and pick the top three or four goals they wish to pursue.

THE SHRINKING EXECUTION PLAN

I keep my Execution Plans for each year, and I have noticed that each year the number of goals we commit to decreases. We have become laser-focused on a few things, and as a result, we have become more capable of achieving our goals. When deciding the strategy for your team, remember, less truly is more.

> *When everything is important, nothing is important.*

At the end of your yearly strategic planning session, you should have three to four company-wide goals. Next, ask your leadership team to decide what is the most important thing their department can contribute in the next ninety days to help achieve the company's yearly goals. Only allow them to commit to three or four department ninety-day sprint goals. (Gino Wickman refers to these sprints as "Rocks.") These department goals should be tactical parts of the yearly strategy that, if achieved, will move you closer to your yearly goal and the company's three- to five-year vision.

When goals are set, make sure they are written in a way that ensures you can tell if they were completed or not by the due date. You probably have heard of a SMART goal, which stands for **S**pecific, **M**easurable, **A**chievable, **R**elevant, and **T**ime-bound. Remember to check each goal with the following question: *How will I know if this goal was achieved?*

"Improve customer service" isn't a SMART goal.

"Within ninety days increase the customer NPS score from 72 to 83" is a SMART goal. Stay away from those unaccountable words like *better*, *improve*, *lower*, and *increase* unless there is a number attached to them.

Next, step out of the way and let your team perform. People don't like to be told what to do, but they do want to know what needs to be done. Most people don't like bosses, but they do like leadership. Your job is to not distract your team from focusing on their goals, which is easier said than done, but nonetheless you should persevere. Your weekly 1-2-1 meetings should be enough time for them to check in and ask for advice, feedback, or help, if needed. The rest of their time they can spend working toward their goals, uninterrupted.

YOUR MUST-WINS

While your team is focused on their ninety-day sprints, you should focus less on the daily running of your business and more on strategic tasks. Before you go to bed at night, or when you wake up each morning, carve out some quiet time to think about what you want to accomplish in a day. During that time, start by reviewing your long-term goals. I have these written on the first page of my journal and look at them each day. After you review your long-term goals, write down your three must-wins for the day.

Must-wins are proactive tasks that you need to complete to reach your long-term goals. You will have busy work to do in the day, but don't confuse busy work with strategic work. Your must-wins should be activities that inch you toward your long-term goals, not busy work. Come hell or high water, you need to focus on finishing your must-wins that day.

Your must-wins should be:

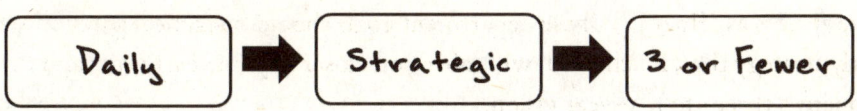

If you walk into the office with a plan, you are less likely to get carried off in the day-to-day current of activities. Having personal, clearly defined must-wins will help you get off the hamster wheel, which makes you feel as though you are working hard while accomplishing little.

What is almost worse than starting your day without a written plan is starting your day with a plan that has twenty tasks on it. Our tendency when we have a long task list is to start on the easy, comfortable items first so we can start checking things off the list. By the end of the day, the three strategic items you were supposed to work on won't get finished. If you need to put twenty tasks on your list, that is fine, but put the three strategic tasks that will move you toward your goal at the top of the list and draw a big line between that and the other tasks. Make sure you finish your must-wins first.

EUREKA CAN WRECK

Sometimes we wake up in the night, rummage for paper in the dark, and jot down an exciting idea. Sometimes an idea will come to us when we are in a meeting, or on our commute to work, or in the shower. Sometimes we are on vacation and finally have a moment to relax and dream. Then, the idea comes like lightning: We have an epiphany, and we march into work like saviors the next day with our idea and a new path for our company. *Eureka! God has spoken! Now let's change the direction of the company's ship.* We are confident this new direction will increase profits and make the company even more successful. We announce this brilliant idea to our team, and our people are excited or nervous about the change.

Everyone switches gears and drops their written goals for the new idea. They stay on the new idea until the owner has his or her next epiphany, and then they drop the new idea for the newer idea and start working on the newer idea, and then the owner has an even better idea and on and on it keeps going. You get the point.

Think carefully before you present any new idea to your team. People listen to their leaders at first, but if their leaders always have ideas and then don't support their ideas with the proper allocation of resources, their team will see these ideas as the flavor of the month.

When I first started leading, we initiated more projects than were possible to finish. My people lacked focus, and it was my fault. I have gotten better at not distracting my team, but it is a constant battle to control my thoughts and to keep my mouth shut. I keep the fight to not distract my team with my ideas front and center in my mind.

Your team needs to focus on doing a few things well instead of doing many things half-assed. If you are running into the office distracting them from their written goals with new ideas, they will never be able to finish what they started. As a leader, you need to focus on not distracting your team from finishing their ninety-day sprints. Take your brilliant ideas and put them in a folder until the next ninety-day sprint meeting. By then, the idea might have lost some of its luster—sometimes a hot, new idea isn't as exciting after you think about it for ninety days.

MY PRECIOUS

Most of my entrepreneurial friends face the same challenge. Each month they come into our business group meetings with a new idea that might improve their business. They turn into Sméagol from *The Lord of the Rings*. They become obsessed, their eyes start popping out of their heads, and they rub their hands together as they think about all the exciting possibilities their precious idea will bring. When they share their new idea, we are all wondering what happened to the exciting idea they talked about last month. We become confused. And if *we* are confused, think about the confusion employees must be experiencing. This is where entrepreneurs fail: They have a new idea each minute, but the execution part is long, tedious, and boring. The execution part is full of boring training, changes in management, and new processes. Entrepreneurs don't do boring well. They like the excitement of new ideas.

New ideas pop up and distract us from getting our ninety-day sprints and yearly goals accomplished. New ideas aren't necessarily bad and sometimes are needed if the economy makes a huge change in the middle of the year, but they still need to be vetted and tactfully put into an Execution Plan.

My dad was a serial entrepreneur who started several businesses in his lifetime. Most of his businesses failed, but even when 3 Men Movers got off the ground, he became bored and was always looking for the next big thing. He would lose focus on the river of cash, the part of our business that brought in the most amount of money, which was our moving business. Like most entrepreneurs, these new ideas are what he lived for and kept him excited.

After he started 3 Men Movers, he also started one of the first mobile phone retail stores in Houston, a landscaping company, a real estate investment company, and a cleaning company—and those are just the businesses I can remember. He grew 3 Men Movers to $3 million in revenue in 2023, but after that he became restless and was looking at the horizon instead of focusing on what was around him.

You won't be likely to grow a scalable business without focus. All the new ideas took my dad's focus away from the river of cash. What is *your* river of cash?

I have learned that deciding what to do isn't just about what you choose to do, as Margaret Cording taught me. It is also about what you choose *not* to do. The word *decide* comes from the Latin word *cide*, which means "to kill off," as we can see in the words *herbicide* and *homicide*. When faced with new ideas, you have to learn to kill off the ones that won't work for you. You have to decide, by killing off ideas that distract so that you can be laser focused on the ones that will make your company successful.

END OF CHAPTER CHECKLIST

- ❑ I defined my river of cash. What my company does better than anyone else in the market.
- ❑ I commit to focusing on my river of cash.
- ❑ I save my new ideas to present to my team during our regularly scheduled quarterly meetings or annual meetings.
- ❑ If an idea is pursued, I will dedicate the time and resources needed to implement the new idea.
- ❑ I have added must-wins to my daily task list that are strategic in nature and push us closer to achieving our long-term goals.
- ❑ I am committing to less goals so that I can focus more resources and time on them to ensure we achieve them.

END OF PART 4 CHECKLIST

- ❏ I have created a one-page Execution Plan that includes the company's mission, core values, vision, yearly goals, and ninety-day sprints. I have made a few tweaks so that it matches what is important in my company.
- ❏ I have communicated my Execution Plan both visually and verbally—as James Brown sang, "Say it loud and say it proud."
- ❏ I hold all staff quarterly meetings to communicate the company's goals. I let people on my team take charge so they gain confidence and learn how to lead.
- ❏ I have a set of core values that are clearly communicated, and I hire and fire based on those core values.
- ❏ Meetings occur regularly with or without me.
- ❏ The meeting agenda is written down and run by the employees.
- ❏ The meetings start and end on time.
- ❏ The meeting is about the company, and we go over key indicators, solve problems, and talk about goals and tasks using accountable language and creating action items using the OCD method.
- ❏ I temper my communication of ideas with my team so I don't derail them from their ninety-day sprints.
- ❏ I structure my week to include my leadership meeting and my 1-2-1 meetings.
- ❏ I have all my meetings scheduled and set up to reoccur on the correct dates.
- ❏ I walk into work with my daily must-wins at the top of my to-do list.
- ❏ I have a digital or paper Idea Folder where I capture my best ideas and introduce them to my team during the yearly strategy meeting.

PART 5

Now What?

22

Now What?

Your company is running smoothly, and you only have to attend a few meetings a week to keep your team on track. Your job now is to stop working on the daily work and to focus on your long-term strategic vision. If you assigned any ninety-day sprints, be sure people are knocking those out, monitor key indicators (your team should be doing this too), and be there for your team when they need you during the week and during your regularly scheduled 1-2-1 meetings.

All this should take less than eight hours per week of disciplined work. It doesn't sound like much, but these hours must be completely structured. As long as you do the legwork from the earlier chapters and follow your structured meeting schedule, you should have more time on your hands to work strategically on your business instead of spending that time putting out fires.

HOW TO SPEND YOUR TIME

If you are used to working forty or more hours a week, what do you do with the rest of your time once you've condensed your essential work into those eight hours? When a company is smaller, sometimes the owner will take on an operational role within the company. He or she might be the top salesperson or manage the books. I started off being an asshole (in the center of everything), and then mostly I worked as an Operations manager until the company grew large enough for me to hire my replacement.

If this is your reality, make sure your name is a part of the process chart with a clear title and bullet-form job description. What you should avoid is overseeing a little bit of everything, which undercuts your managers' authority. Be careful that you don't slip back into the center of everything. If that happens, you will fall into being the office asshole.

Your empowered team should start being accountable, instead of being held accountable. They will stop needing your feedback several times a day and be able to work toward their goal without constant supervision.

If you have accountable people on your team and are following your meeting schedule, you should resist following up with your team on projects and tasks between meetings. Asking whether an important customer called is OK. Asking your manager daily about an important ninety-day sprint is micromanaging.

Countless studies show that people like autonomy at work. Let them have it. You will be able to coach and help them during your weekly 1-2-1 and during the weekly leadership meeting. Trust them enough to know that they will seek you out if they need help. If monitoring certain key indicators is important to you, then ask your team members to create an automated report to send to you with daily key indicators so you won't have to bug them for this information. Your employees should be focused on the company's goals and not focused on pleasing you.

If you are not riding your team's asses all day, what are you doing? I research innovative ideas, work on strategy, establish key business relationships, police and promote our brand through community outreach, and stay updated on and involved in my industry. I also work on special projects that are outside our company's daily workflow, such as buying a new warehouse or testing new software. And—don't tell my team—but I am constantly looking at new ideas. I just try not to distract my team with them, so I keep my ideas to myself until we have our quarterly meeting.

If an issue arises, I make a point of having crucial conversations with my direct reports. Hopefully, most of the conversations should occur during my

1-2-1s. When I arrive at work, I think, *Whom do I need to talk to today?* For me, usually, that person is the person I least wanted to speak with because I am averse to confrontation, but nonetheless such people are always the people I need to speak to first.

MANAGE BY WALKING AROUND

If you don't know your people, and you don't know what is happening on the floor, how do you know your company? Your team can spot insincerity a mile away, so you have to feel it and genuinely care about them and not just go through the motions. Practice MBWA (Management by Walking Around). Make connections with your people. If your people don't know who you are, they will create an idea, accurate or not, of who they think you are (I learned this the hard way). As you grow, it will become more of a challenge to have close relationships with every person on your team.

Now, with many people working in remote offices, instead of walking around, arrange virtual coffee dates with your people. Make sure that the dates stay positive. Bring good news with you to share. If you ask someone to have coffee with you and then you launch at them with critical feedback of what they are doing wrong, they will dread the next time you ask to meet them for coffee. Give feedback only during the 1-2-1 meetings. Save coffee dates for getting to know your employee and how they are doing at work and at home if they are comfortable sharing.

When I had to get my kids to school at the crack of dawn, I drove straight to work right after I dropped them off, arriving while the morning skeleton crew was working. I would make my coffee and then go into Operation's dispatch area, and because there was no place for a visitor to sit, I would sit on the floor, and my customer service manager, Norma, and dispatcher, Arny, would turn their chairs toward me, after which we would have a five- to ten-minute chat each morning. I enjoyed these intimate talks before the rest of the team arrived. We often talked about family life and weekend plans. It was good for all of us to get to know each other on a personal level. They learned that I was not just their "boss," but an ordinary person worried about the same shit we all are worried about. Breaking down the barrier made it easier for them to come to me when they needed help. To this day the three of us feel very bonded, and

I am sure it stems from the time we invested getting to know each other during our early morning coffee chats many years ago.

Make time daily to have these moments of communication with your team. Although it may seem like discussing nonwork-related topics is a waste of time, building a relationship and trust with your team is essential to your success.

PERCEPTION IS REALITY

When I started managing 3 Men Movers, several people on my team would say that they used to think I was mean, and it wasn't until they got to know me that they realized I actually was really nice. They meant it as a compliment, but I was crushed when I received this feedback.

I'm an intense person. I grew up in an intense home and had lots of responsibilities thrust upon me at an early age. I examined my behavior and realized that I walked through the office many mornings in deep thought with a frown on my face, ignoring people who walked by me and greeted me—so lost in thought that I had tunnel vision and didn't even notice anyone's existence. Sometimes, I walked in with a cell phone glued to my ear, perhaps in a heated discussion with a vendor. Although I was never directly mean to anyone, these behaviors gave the impression to my team that I was aloof or that I thought I was too important to even say "Hi." Whether or not this was my intention is irrelevant; their perception was their reality and their truth, and I was behaving like a jerk.

I decided that these were little things that were easy to fix. Now when I arrive to work in the morning, I end my business and personal calls prior to entering the office and walk in while greeting everyone with a smile and a "Hello." I am also now cognizant of smiling and saying "Hi" to people when I pass them in the hall. For some of you this might come naturally, but it doesn't feel natural to me because I am an introverted person. These behavior changes have made a difference in how my team perceives me.

As a leader, all eyes are on you first thing in the morning. Your team will comment to each other, "Watch out, he is in a bad mood." Or, "Looks like it is going to be a long day." Do you appear to be angry? Do you walk in while on the phone, upset with the auto mechanic because they are dragging their feet on finishing your repairs, only to have every person on your team worried about how it will affect their day?

Perhaps you coach your customer service team to keep their baggage at home and don't let the customers see them in a bad mood.

> **When you are in a leadership position, your team members are your customers.**

When you show up at work, show up as the best version of you. When you walk in the office, it is showtime. Emotions are not necessarily a bad thing, but use them to ignite people around a cause or bring people in close to an idea. Control your emotions and use them as tools; don't let your emotions control you.

END OF CHAPTER REVIEW

A list of the differences between what small business leaders work on during a normal workday compared to what midsized business leaders work on appears on page 202. Review the list and see if you are working on small business work or mid to large business work.

SMALL BUSINESS	MIDSIZE BUSINESS (AND GROWING!)
Profitability from a sale	Tracking quarterly and yearly earnings
Sales transactions with customer	Creating a long-term growth strategy
Fixing daily issues	Troubleshooting long-term processes
Accounting daily entries	Analyzing financial reports
Daily work	Creating future ideas to expand, products, markets
Personnel issues	Mentoring personnel to greatness
Solving problems, line at your door	Regularly scheduling 1-2-1s
Spontaneously announcing new ideas	Creating 90-day sprints and yearly goals
Accepting "unaccountable" language	Assigning all tasks OCD
Setting deadlines for your team	Allowing team members to set their own goals
Constantly following up on tasks	Following up only during scheduled meetings

WHAT SMALL BUSINESS OWNERS FOCUS ON VS. WHAT MATURE BUSINESS OWNERS FOCUS ON

23

Losing Money to Make Money

Steve Jobs spent countless hours in a room at Apple called the "packing room." This was the room where they designed packaging for Apple products. There were hundreds of different prototypes made from varied materials. The final design for the iPhone box was even granted a patent. They went so far as to make sure that the box made a *whoosh* sound when you slid the lid off. Why would a CEO of a large organization be so involved in a cardboard box?

Brand.

Jobs understood that only *brand* separates your products or services from being a commodity. Without your brand, you are competing on price. What exactly is brand?

A brand is the promise that you make to your customers.

Brand can be a mystical idea that is everywhere and nowhere all at once. A brand can be a promise like Walmart's: *to give their customers the lowest price.* A brand can be a promise like Disney's: *to give their customers a magical experience*. A brand can be about a promise of uncompromising luxury, like Mercedes's. When I bought 3 Men Movers, it had no assets—its value was based on its successful business model and the 3 Men Movers' brand.

As an owner of a large company, you must be the brand ambassador for your company. It is easy to get comfortable with letting all of your employees run the show, but some of them might be new and not have an intimate understanding of your brand. While in a company's Maturity Phase, you should not be micromanaging the day-to-day work; you should always be aware of anything that harms your company's brand and be ready to step in if noticed. You have to be vocal and make sure that the company's brand is always on point. Being a brand ambassador is still one of your most important jobs.

YOU HAVE A BRAND

Whether you have a written defined brand or not, you have a brand. I knew a man whose company was the only place you could find a specific type of specialized parts. Customers were forced to deal with him in order to get his parts—"forced" because he was also known for having horrible customer service. He was a sweet guy but was overwhelmed and didn't have proper processes to follow up on his customers' requests.

I was in a business group with the guy, and he wanted to know how he could improve his business. We asked around the marketplace to see what people thought about his brand and heard the same answer repeatedly: His unwritten brand was "Exclusive parts from a company that is slow at delivering them." In his case, people had no option but to buy from him due to the limited number of companies who carried this unique product. In the open market, consumers have a choice.

We decided to see our brand from our customers' point of view, so we created a survey, then employed word-cloud software to show us the most repeated words our customers used to describe our services. You don't see *cheap*, because our brand is not based on price.

I discovered one of my favorite examples of *brand differentiation* while walking through the grocery store. There were two brands of salt sitting next to each other on the shelf: Morton's with the logo of the lady under the umbrella, and another cost cutter brand with "NON-IODIZED SALT" in big black letters

amazing arrived awesome belongings best **careful**
company **courteous** customer definitely done easy
efficient everyone everything excellent
experience extremely fantastic **fast friendly** furniture
guys hard **helpful** highly items **job** needed nice
office polite **professional** prompt quick
quickly really **recommend** respectful **service** staff
super **team thank** things timely took used **worked**

on the front of the yellow container. The Morton's brand was twice the price. There was absolutely no difference in the product except for the Morton's label. One wasn't a special kosher salt, or a pink salt, or a salt from the Black Sea. Morton's didn't have expensive, special packaging. They were two containers of plain old salt. My knee-jerk reaction was to reach for the Morton's without thinking. Why would anyone pay twice the amount for the exact same product?

Because they are familiar with the name and logo, and they trust the brand.

As a business owner, you should spend a significant amount of your time clearly defining your brand and protecting it at all costs from internal and external threats.

Internal Threat. An example of an internal threat is an employee who doesn't understand your brand. If your brand is based on offering "amazing customer service" and, instead of giving that kind of service, your employees are rude and disrespectful to your customers, you're facing an internal threat. Another example would be showing your brand online in a way that doesn't represent your brand. If your brand is all about "family values" and you have pictures on your social media of employees getting wild at a company party, well, that isn't in line with your brand either.

External Threat. An example of an external threat is anything that erodes your brand outside your company. This could come from a news program doing an exposé on your company or a customer or competitor saying something negative online. While it is impossible to prevent all external threats, you should take each one seriously and work on minimizing the fallout.

A tarnish of your brand could be disastrous to overcome. If you are old enough, you might remember back in the 1980s when someone poisoned some bottles of Tylenol. At first, nobody knew how it happened and if it was an isolated case. Tylenol could have taken their product off the shelves in the city where the cases of poisoning happened, but the company didn't, instead absorbing the expense of taking every single bottle of Tylenol off the shelf throughout the US. The company was open and transparent in the way it handled the situation, doing whatever it could to protect the brand. The recall cost the company millions of dollars, yet the expensive recall was money well spent protecting the brand. Despite the scandal that took place years ago, Tylenol is still such a trusted brand today that most parents wouldn't hesitate to give Tylenol to their feverish child.

What is the value of your brand and how much are you willing to spend protecting it? We have all heard that if a customer receives good service, they tell a few people about it, but when they receive bad service, they tell *everyone*. In today's environment with the advent of social media, this is more relevant than ever. Take, for example, when United Airlines got on the wrong side of a musician named Dave Carroll. Apparently, the airline's baggage handlers threw around his custom-made guitar and broke it. United refused to do anything to rectify the situation and gave Carroll the runaround. Being a musician, Dave Carroll wrote a song entitled "United Breaks Guitars" to vent his frustration and posted it on YouTube in July 2009, hitting number one on iTunes after a few weeks, and within a few months he had five million views. After a few years, he had ten million views, and as of 2020, he had fifteen million views. It was a public relations nightmare for United Airlines, who still uses this example for customer service training today.

In the United Airlines case, a man's rant through a song went viral. On a smaller scale, you can calculate the cost of tarnishing your brand by not honoring your brand's promise at a customer level.

BECOME A FANATIC

Consider the lifetime value of your customer: If your product costs $500 and people will purchase six units in their lifetime, that is $500 x 6 = $3,000. This is the amount a person will spend in their lifetime on your goods or services. If you upset a customer early in your business relationship, you could potentially lose the entire lifetime value of that customer.

Now say, according to the research from the White House Office of Consumer Affairs, that unhappy customers usually tell between nine and fifteen people. Let's be conservative and say your unhappy customer tells nine people. Not only will you lose your customer for life; you will also lose the nine other people for life, the ones your customer tells about their horrible experience.

If you do the math, that is 10 (your customer plus their friends and family) x $3,000 = $30,000, and the number continues to grow if those ten people in turn tell more people about the original customer's negative experience.

When you look at the big picture, losing a little money on a single job to honor your brand and delight your customer is the soundest business decision for the long run. Customers venting on the Internet can have a ripple effect that dwarfs the equations above, and one negative review can potentially reach millions of potential buyers causing them to choose a competitor over you.

Protecting your brand involves making sure your product or service is clearly defined and stays within that definition. Small business owners who are desperate to make money often try to branch out into diverse types of goods and services so that they can be everything to everyone. Their reasoning is that, by saying yes to everything, they are casting a wider net to capture more revenue. While the idea might sound good, being everything to everyone only dilutes your brand. A customer at Saks Fifth Avenue wouldn't want to see a $35 pair of Crocs rubber sandals in the shoe department, and a customer at Walmart wouldn't want to see a $1,350 pair of Prada heels in the shoe aisle. Ask yourself the following: *What can my company be the* best *at in the market?* Then align your brand with that answer.

With access to so many homeowners at various times over the history of running the company, I decided that we should start trying to sell electricity, landscaping, and cleaning services. Yes, we could do it all—we just couldn't be the very best at it. What we could be the best at is moving people, and when we sell goods and products within *that* specific vertical, we have always been successful. All these other ideas I chased throughout the early years took my team's focus away from the river of cash, which for us was our relocation services. We can be the best movers in the industry.

Every company should sit down and create brand guidelines for their company, which should be distributed throughout the company to ensure compliance. I used to feel guilty for being so picky about how the 3 Men Movers' brand was represented, but now I realize that it is OK to be fanatical about a company brand. As an owner, being a brand fanatic was my job.

My Marketing team ensures that our brand is always shown in the best possible light. These guidelines describe everything from the color and style of our logo, to the fonts we use in written documents, to the way our teams are shown in pictures. We want our company always to be displayed at its best. Our people are always shown to be happy and smiling. You will never see a dirty truck on social media or on the road. But a brand encompasses much more than just the Pantone colors on your company logo.

Your brand is the promise you make to your customers. What is your brand?

END OF CHAPTER CHECKLIST

- ❑ I have defined my brand.
- ❑ I have also defined what my brand is not.
- ❑ I have a set of brand guidelines for my team to follow.
- ❑ I am following my brand on all social media sites.
- ❑ I have done a brand audit; I know what my brand reputation is online.
- ❑ If possible, I am often a customer of my own products and services and insist on being a customer with no special treatment so I get to experience my company from a customer's perspective.
- ❑ I speak up immediately if I notice that the way my brand is being portrayed seems "off" to ensure that it gets back on track quickly.
- ❑ I am willing to lose money when it comes to protecting my brand.
- ❑ I am a fanatic when it comes to my company's brand.

24

To the Victor Goes the Spoils

In business school you learn that a company's number one goal is to "increase shareholders' earnings." Most businesses in the US are privately owned; therefore, the shareholder is the business owner, and the earnings are the profits of the business. Does this mean that the goal in business is to make the owner rich?

If so, this seems like a shitty way for employees to spend their days. What's in it for them? Even with a great work environment and excellent perks, the team members you are going into battle with will want to share in the spoils.

WHAT THE MARKET BEARS

Shortly after COVID-19 hit, I was in the Florida Keys on a vacation. I overheard the attendant at a small shop say that he was enjoying the traveling restrictions that were in place. When people were not shopping, he had a lot less work to do. He was getting paid the same amount but without having to deal with a huge crowd. When crowds are large, the owner of the store makes more money, but the employee who is doing more work makes the same amount. While you would hope the employee made the connection that more customers equates to more profits and in turn that means the business is healthy and he has job security, he wasn't thinking about the big picture. His thoughts, which are also logical, were: *More work for the same money. This sucks!* If his company had a profit-share plan in place, then he and the owner of the shop would have aligned incentives. If he had to service more customers to help the company hit its goals, he would make more money too!

I have a great group of employees. People look at my team and think I must pay my staff way above market rate. I don't, and I don't believe you should either. 3 Men Movers has been in business for over thirty years and has made it through economic swings, the biggest one being the housing crash of 2007. The moving industry rises and falls with home sales, and the housing crash hit the moving industry hard. Several multigenerational movers went out of business. In times like these, if you are paying above market rates, you will be forced to either do a layoff or salary reduction, neither of which is good for morale.

Oil and gas companies pay over market rates to their employees and end up having massive layoffs to reduce expenses when oil prices fall. Why not instead pay your employees market rate and give out large bonuses during the years that you hit profit goals?

Instead of having an inflated payroll that only can be supported if you bring in huge revenue numbers, only share the spoils of war when you are victorious and hit your goals. To do this, create a profit-sharing pool for all employees to share when the company goals are met. Instead of a high portion of your payroll being fixed, the bonus portion is variable and adjusts with profits. You pay your team a big bonus when they are doing a great job and the economy is booming, and if the economy takes a hit, your team still gets their market salary.

When deciding on how much to allocate to bonuses, don't get stingy here—after all, what do you have to lose? Your team will only make the big bucks when the company hits home runs. Our bonuses in good years are sometimes as high as our employees' salaries for the year. Why be cheap? If your team helps you hit your numbers, everyone should win.

FOCUS ON THE LIVABLE WAGE

My dad never had a job that paid him well. When he started 3 Men Movers, he wanted to make sure that his people were decently paid. Nobody on your team should make less than a living wage unless they have a part-time intern position—and even then, I think interns should get paid. After all, you get what you pay for. If your teammates are not making enough to provide essentials for their families, then they will not be able to focus and give you their best work.

If your business model is such that you can't afford to pay an employee a livable wage, then your business model is broken. There is nothing worse for an employee than to struggle to pay their rent and know that the owner of the company is off on another ski trip with their family. Working forty hours a week and being unable to take care of your family is demoralizing. Studies show that making a high amount of money won't make someone happier, but making less than a living wage will make someone depressed.

Create a company that you would want your son or daughter to work for. Wouldn't you want them to have time off to care for your newborn grandchild? Wouldn't you want them to have healthcare and make enough money to live comfortably?

I grew up in a house where both my parents worked full-time and yet we could barely pay the bills. I watched my parents struggle. Nobody should go through what my parents and many other Americans go through. If your employees are working full-time and qualify for food stamps, then that is an issue that needs to be addressed immediately. People deserve better.

END OF CHAPTER CHECKLIST

- ❑ I have analyzed payroll and compared it with industry reports to ensure that I am paying market rates. (Utilizing IBIS reports for your industry is a good place to start.)
- ❑ I have looked at the living wage in my area to ensure that everyone on my staff is at least making that amount. (Utilizing livingwage.mit.edu calculator is a good place to start.)
- ❑ I have devised a plan so that everyone on my team can make more money if we hit our goals. I have shared that plan with my employees. The plan is achievable.

25
Change Is the Only Constant

The market is changing, customers' needs are changing, technology is changing, our competition is changing, and if your company doesn't change, it will be left behind in the marketplace.

When owning a moving company, every day you get to be with people while they experience one of the biggest changes in their lives: changing where they live. Moving is hard on people. A person attaches memories to the place they call home. When they leave that place, they don't just abandon the physical space of the four walls and roof—they feel the loss of disconnecting from a place filled with nostalgia.

Although a move can be an exciting time, there is also a feeling of loss; a move is a mark in time and signifies that life is marching forward. You will no longer be in the home where your child took their first steps or where you shared your last meal with your parents. Even the nicest person in the world gets testy on their move day. Combined with the utter exhaustion of packing and preparing for their move, they must deal with changing their entire home environment. I have learned from being involved in hundreds of thousands of moves that the best way to keep people calm during this time of change is to make sure there are no surprises. If people are aware of what will happen ahead of time, they will be mentally prepared to handle even the worst situations.

Clear and open communication is important. Sometimes we are accused of *over*communicating, but one of our mottos is that surprises are for birthdays and not move days.

YOUR CHANGING COMPANY

A company that is experiencing hyper-growth is also experiencing change. And the changes are coming at you and your employees fast. Change affects people differently. Some people who are easily adaptable, like me, absolutely love change. I will fix things that aren't broken just to be doing something new and different, an impulse that I have to keep in check. People who embrace change are people who like to travel to exotic places and try strange foods. They rejoice in the new, different, and unusual. They are the first adopters of new technologies and aren't afraid of automation.

Most people don't like changes, and that is why there are whole fields of study, departments within large companies, and books written about change management. Most people go to the same restaurants and order the same meal every week because they feel safe that way, a habit that descends from prehistoric ancestors who noted whether or not someone died after drinking from a watering hole. Not dying meant success, so you would go back to that one watering hole instead of trying a new place. If you sat next to caveman Frank, and he didn't kill you, you were cool with Frank. But here comes caveman Joe, and you have never met Joe before. Seeing caveman Joe would heighten your fear. Joe could have a club and kill you.

It is a natural human instinct to fear strangers and new things. Therefore, it is difficult when new managers are brought in and when companies change strategic directions.

CHANGE, EMOTIONS, AND LOSS

Psychologists claim that change triggers the same emotional phases as the loss of a loved one. Even something as seemingly benign as installing a new software system can cause someone to go through the same stages of grief as a death in the family.

Denial: "I can't believe they bought this technology. I am sure it won't last."

Anger: "Management is always wasting money upgrading technology. This crap is just making my job more complicated."

Bargaining: "I wonder if we get together and have a meeting with management, maybe they will let some of us stay on the old system."

Depression: "Damn, I have no choice but to learn this stupid software. This sucks!"

Acceptance: "Well, maybe it isn't so bad."

If new software can stir up so many emotions, think about the effects of a new supervisor, commission structure, or process. If you are running a company that is undergoing exponential growth, some people within your organization will not be able to keep up. As a leader, you must do what you can to help people transition to keep up with the company's growth.

INCREASING COMMUNICATION AND TRAINING

How do you combat the anxiety-filled ripple that change causes throughout your organization?

- **Engage in open, transparent communication.** You can't always share everything with your employees, especially when you are not 100 percent sure what the future holds. As soon as you do have clarity, communicate with your team. Even if at times things don't look good, transparency is usually the best policy. People want to know what is going to happen and how it will directly affect them. Always communicate with your team the worst possible scenario because once they know you are always honest about change, you will earn your team's trust.
- **Increase the knowledge and skills of your team through continuous training.** If your employees do not have the skills to be able to operate in the company you will grow to become, you need to create a plan to get them the skills they need as quickly as possible. Current employees may lack skills, but they make up for it by having a solid understanding of your culture and values, the essence and fabric of what makes

your company special. Good people are hard to come by, so if you have good people on your team, invest in them to increase their skills so that they can grow alongside your growing company.

Some employees come with their own personal baggage. Maybe they have issues with trust stemming from childhood. Maybe the management at their last job did them wrong. When you introduce something new, they may perceive it as a possible threat instead of seeing changes as positive actions to spur or support growth. Hiring a new manager, instituting a new compensation plan, or implementing a new process can all affect people in negative ways if precautions are not taken.

One of my biggest breakthroughs was with an employee named Claudia. Every time we would change something she became racked with angst. I would have to talk her down from a full-blown panic attack. She has worked with me for over fifteen years and basically grew up in the company. Recently, I overheard her tell another team member, "Don't worry. When things change, I have learned that it always gets better." I never believed those words would come out of her mouth. I literally asked her if she was feeling all right, and she just smiled. It took her a while, but she learned to trust the company.

I read lots of business books: Most of them only tell stories about success. CEOs write about how things work out and how all their employees fall in line and love everything about their companies. Unfortunately, this isn't the real world. Even the best business will make bad hires or have disgruntled employees. Even the best employees might be perfect for the company you are today, but not a fit for the company you are becoming. In this case they will normally opt out and quit.

Once, I brought a new manager onto my team, and one of my employees didn't trust her, which by itself might not have posed a long-term problem because some people take longer to process change. But the employee also began challenging the manager during meetings, pushing back on the proposed direction, pointing out why the new plan wouldn't work, and so on. This type of behavior isn't entirely out of the norm, and you may very well experience it as you add new people to your team as your company grows.

While inexperienced managers can become stressed when a person on their team challenges them at a group meeting—it can be embarrassing to be called out in front of a group—this is something I like. Being challenged in front of a group used to stress me out, but now I have come to think that being challenged during a group meeting is actually an opportunity. Here is why:

- **It shows that they trust you enough to raise issues.** If you bring up a controversial change and everyone nods and doesn't ask questions, chances are they are too afraid to tell you their real concerns.
- **The courageous people who are willing to challenge you are probably asking the questions others are thinking but are too afraid to bring up.** It is better to clear the air in a group so that everyone can get the information they need.
- **If you are challenged and you stay calm, your credibility as a leader increases.** Leaders are supposed to be strong and not get rattled. Also, it is OK to say, "I don't know." You don't always have to have all the answers. If you don't know, commit to finding out and letting your team know as soon as you find out the answers they need.
- **The number of items that need to be talked about in the second meeting decreases.** The second meeting is the informal meeting your staff has with each other—you won't be invited—in which they hash out what you said at the first meeting in more depth and add their own opinions and interpretations.

We are aware of employees who have issues with change and make sure to provide extra help in any transition. But there are behaviors that aren't repairable. For example, this particular employee tried, after the first and second meeting, to rally others to try to undermine the company's goals. Even though the employee was a top performer and I had to take a temporary financial hit, I let him go. If I had not let him go, the financial hit could have been greater because he was working on eroding the values we had worked so hard to establish.

This employee no doubt falls into The Untouchable quadrant: Low Attitude and High Aptitude. Untouchables do not support a company's growth.

I don't like firing anyone. I consider it a personal failure: It means that we hired wrong, or something went off track along the way to get us to this point. But not everyone will be able to make it in a growing company. Your job as an owner is to grow your company while not leaving too many bodies in the wake of that trajectory.

END OF CHAPTER CHECKLIST

- ❑ Identify people on your team who need extra nurturing during times of change.
- ❑ Create a way to communicate all changes to your team. Huddles and departmental meetings are a great way to notify teams of changes. Having 1-2-1 meetings prior to the group meetings is a great way to share changes with people on your team who take a while to adapt to changes. Make sure you use several methods to communicate, including in-person meetings, online chats, emails, and bulletin boards.
- ❑ Make sure people on your team have resources that can support them during a big change, especially someone who will listen to them in a nonjudgmental way and help them during these times.

26

It's All Your Fault!

Years ago, we had a manager who had a hot temper and was always walking into my office to complain about his direct reports. He was full of energy and enthusiasm but could run hot and cold. "They don't care . . . I have asked them to do their job, and they are not listening . . . They didn't finish . . ." After listening to him vent one last time, I said, "If your team is so bad, maybe you need to consider replacing some of them."

He was taken aback. He didn't want to fire anyone; he only needed to vent. But the experience got me thinking about his reasons for being frustrated. First, the issues he was having with his direct reports were his fault. Managers are 100 percent responsible for their people, so in my eyes, this was his problem and not theirs. Either he was not an effective manager if he was having recurring issues or he had the wrong people on his team. Since he was allowed to hire and fire people on his team, fixing these issues would be his responsibility.

When I got home that day, I continued to contemplate his situation. It occurred to me that his people not performing well was ultimately *my* fault for hiring him. Either I needed to mentor and train him so that he could get better performance from his team, or I needed to find a better person for this management position. His direct reports messing up was completely my fault.

As a leader, every single thing that goes wrong within your organization can be directly linked to *you*. I know it is easier and more comfortable to not take personal responsibility for problems within your organization. You get home and complain to your spouse that your Sales manager is incompetent or the lead person you assigned to a project is useless. But guess what: You hired them. Or you hired the manager who hired them. If they are showing up every day and getting a paycheck by doing substandard work, who is the incompetent one?

It may sound confusing that while you are expected *to be responsible for everything*, you are not supposed *to be in the middle of everything*. This doesn't mean *you* have to do all the work or micromanage your team. As a business owner, you are supposed to ensure that you have the right people and processes in place to achieve your mission statement while working within your unique core values.

PROBLEM-SOLVING

Let me walk you through the processes of how to solve a problem at work.

1. **Ask yourself if the issue is a Black Swan event.** You don't want to waste your time making elaborate plans to fix an issue that, if we looked more closely, turned out to be an event that is so rare that it might not ever happen again. These are Black Swan events. You can do a quick fix to patch the current situation, but you don't need to worry about changing a person or process. These are the only times you can excuse yourself from culpability. A Black Swan event is like a meteor hitting the earth: impossible to predict and rare.
2. **If it isn't a Black Swan event, decide if it is a broken process or lack of a process.** If you can fix or add an appropriate process, do so. If an employee is following the process perfectly and the outcome creates an issue, then it is a broken process that needs to be fixed.
3. **If the process is good, find out why the employee didn't follow the process.** Was it will or skill?
    a. *Will*. Did the employee just not want to follow the process? If it was will, you need to get the employee onboard with the process,

and if they can't get onboard, then you need to offboard them from your payroll.

b. *Skill.* If the employee didn't have adequate training, then it was skill. Maybe the employee was careless. Certain processes will have a slight error ratio, which is normal if it is a repeated process. In this situation of an employee not having the skill, you will need to invest in more training to ensure he/she improves. If the employee doesn't improve with the proper training, they might not have the capacity to do their job.

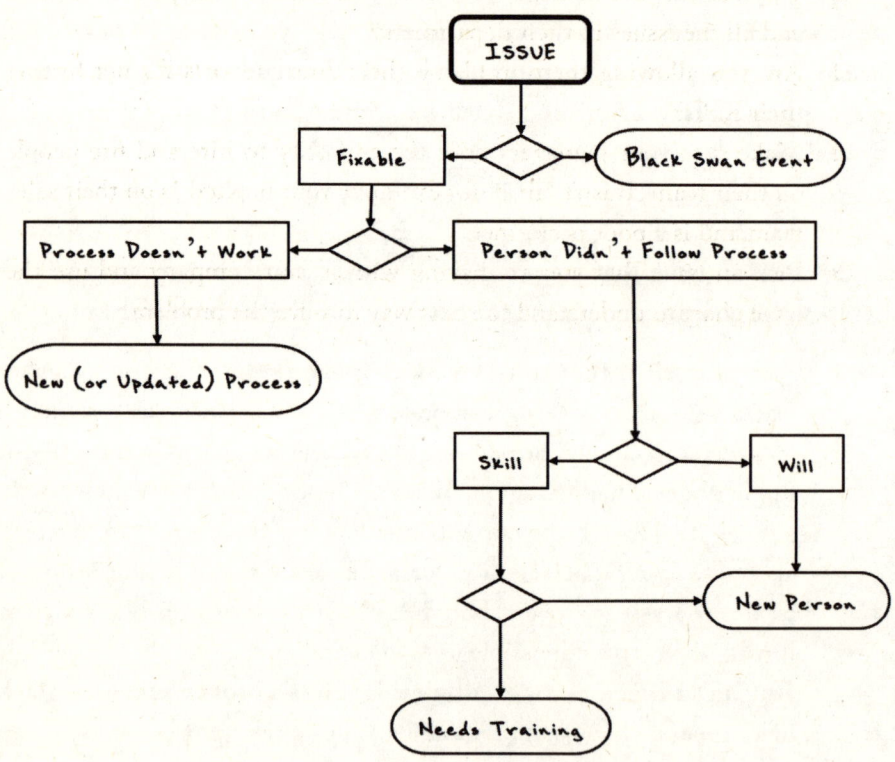

PROBLEM-SOLVING FLOWCHART

As a leader and business owner, it is your responsibility to hire competent people, create effective processes, and to monitor these processes with KPIs. You are responsible for hiring competent managers too. Your managers are also responsible for hiring competent people and creating effective processes. A mistake must be investigated and used as an opportunity to better understand your people and processes so you can make improvements within your organization. Remember the following: The first time you are a victim; the second time you are a volunteer.

Ultimately, each problem can be followed up the organizational structure to you and your ability to hire the right people and implement the right processes.

END OF CHAPTER CHECKLIST

- ❑ Think about your managers. Do they take accountability for their KPIs and all the issues in their department?
- ❑ Are you allowing them to blame their direct reports for not hitting their KPIs?
- ❑ Make sure your managers have the authority to hire and fire people on their team. It isn't fair if, for example, your nephew is on their sales team and is a poor performer.
- ❑ Pick an issue that you are having within your company and use the issue chart to understand the best way to solve the problem.

27

Experience Not Necessary

Business owners should have some sort of mentorship in place to advise them. Whether you receive mentorship through an organization such as a business group, or through an experienced business coach, or through another business owner who is willing to take you on, it is important to have a resource to turn to for high-level problem-solving. Good mentorship is the only substitute for lack of experience. Yes, you can read books like this one to help you with your company, but there is no substitute for being able to solve real issues in real time with a peer.

One of the best actions I took when starting off in business was to join the business group Vistage, which provided me with a sounding board of seasoned business professionals. It was like having my own board of directors to help me solve important issues. It isn't cheap, and it was a bit of a financial stretch to pay the monthly fees when I first joined. Sometimes I would sit through our monthly eight-hour meeting for seven hours and fifty-five minutes and not learn a thing, but even in those meetings, I achieved at least five minutes of clarity: a small, golden nugget of knowledge that made the time and membership dues worthwhile.

Every month, I get at least one idea that can increase my profits by a percentage point or two or that improves the quality of my life or my team's or the quality of service I provide my customers. I have been lucky to be a part of a core group that has stuck together for years. Whether you join Vistage or another business group, just make sure that your group follows a set agenda and is composed of people you respect: Developing trust over time with the people within your group will help you feel safe to be vulnerable, so you can let your guard down and share challenging issues.

IT GETS LONELY

Being a business owner can be lonely. Not only does good mentorship act as a sounding board when you have issues, it also creates camaraderie to help you avoid feeling isolated. You are around people all day, and yet you have to keep your communication measured and tempered. You can't tell your Operations manager, "Hey, I think these new regulations might be the end of us." You shouldn't share with your employees your uncertainty about the company's direction. You can't express some of your biggest fears. Unless you are married to an entrepreneur, it is hard for your spouse to understand the stress—and your spouse might just get sick of hearing about everything.

Employees worry about their paycheck; as a business owner, you worry about making payroll for the entire company. A mentoring group or a mentor is a better outlet when you need to discuss issues, and its members have the shared experience of entrepreneurship to help guide you in the right direction.

TOM LOBER

Tom Lober, a member of my Vistage group, was about eighteen years older than me and owned a party boat rental company. People would charter his boats for weddings or work retreats, and he would serve them great food with a DJ playing music while cruising off the Gulf Coast. Over the years, we became friends. When the Internet became a big thing, he mentored me on how to use Google to get leads and explained the ins and outs of online advertising. He had a challenging business model because people hopefully only get married once, and with work parties, they like to try new venues each year. There wasn't a lot of repeat demand for his party boats—he was constantly looking for new ways to conjure up business.

Tom had a restaurant owner's personality: He was a gracious host, with an easy smile, who was a good storyteller and a great listener. During one meeting, he raised a new issue: He wanted to take a year off and travel the world, so he wanted to get into a position so that his business could run itself while he was gone. Everyone thought he was crazy, but that is what he wanted, so we brainstormed strategies for him to make that happen.

After he found someone to run his company, he took off to travel the world. These were trips of a lifetime to China, Russia, and Australia, sometimes with his adult children in tow. When he returned, his storytelling ability didn't disappoint. He told us about the time he sailed solo from Florida to Bimini on a thirty-five-foot catamaran. The boat nearly capsized as it was caught on an underwater line. He was in the middle of the ocean, at night, in the dark, alone and in a dangerous situation. He tied a rope around himself and attached it to the boat to prevent the current from sweeping him away. Then he jumped over the side with an underwater light and a knife. He was able to find what the boat was caught on—a lobster trap—which he proceeded to cut away after diving below the boat in darkness.

We were on the edge of our seats listening to the story and asked, "Tom, what did you do next?"

He replied, "Pulled up the trap, poured a glass of cabernet, and had lobster for dinner, of course!" He was the model of adventurousness balanced by practicality.

After Tom's yearlong sabbatical, he went back to work. He was an avid runner who had run several marathons, but he started having some back pain, which he ignored. Our Vistage chair, Robin Stanaland, finally pushed Tom to have his back checked out by a doctor, who diagnosed him with cancer. After being admitted to the hospital, he learned that the cancer had spread throughout his body, which resulted in a prognosis of just a few months to live.

Tom was facing his own mortality, was worried about his children, and needed to figure out what he was going to do with his company, which was difficult to run. He needed help. The first person he reached out to was Robin. He asked Robin if she would get together a small group of people from our Vistage team to help him for the next few months.

I was one of the members who was picked to be on his special support team. On a Wednesday, Robin called me to tell me that Tom was dying. Our small team was to assemble the next day at the hospital to talk to him about his needs. We were ready to do everything in our ability to help our friend.

On Thursday, I drove to the hospital and met the rest of the group in the hall outside his hospital room. The doctor came out of Tom's room with a somber expression and told us that our dear friend Tom's organs had already begun to shut down, and the prognosis had changed. Instead of having a few months to live, the doctor said he only had a few days left. He had just given Tom the bad news. We all looked at each other, speechless. How could we face Tom and be strong for him when we were having trouble processing the news ourselves?

We walked into the room. Tom was in the hospital bed looking weak and pale. He was dying. This adventurous, amazing man would be no more in a matter of days. I walked over and sat next to the bed and held his hand. I smiled, and he tried to speak, but he was breathless, and I could barely hear his words. It was as if he had run a marathon, and now he was at the end.

In a whisper, he apologized for not being able to speak. I said, "Don't worry, Tom, you talk too much anyway, and I never get to get a word in so now it is my turn to speak." At that, he smiled. "I love you," I told him, "and thank you for all the help and support you have given me throughout the years. Thank you so much." I squeezed his hand gently and then moved aside so the next person could say their goodbyes. We left the room in a state of shock. I would never see Tom again.

Tom went to the doctor on a Monday and died on a Sunday. We were not able to spend the next few months working on a plan with him to transition his company. Unfortunately, his time had run out. His daughter ended up taking over his company and joining our group. We certainly knew where the bodies were buried in his business. We knew about his approach to marketing, and we understood his employees. We were able to help his daughter run the business and then later sell it, after which she bought a large catamaran, and following in her father's footsteps, she set off to sail around the world with her husband. As I write this, they are somewhere near Asia.

That is the power of being in a good business group: You don't simply gain friends—you have loyal comrades.

BUSINESS GROUP LESSONS

I have learned that the people who need mentorship the most are the people who end up leaving the group. Most of the time, these are the ones whose businesses operate with an asshole structure. During our monthly group meeting, these are the people who come late and leave early because they have more important things to do. Their phones go off throughout our meetings, and they constantly check their messages. They are so busy being the company assholes that they can't work strategically on their companies.

I also learned that if you are afraid to be vulnerable, you won't get much from a group. Some members initially show up to brag about how they have it all together or tell us about the next big idea that is going to make them millions. They are afraid to bring up real issues and admit that they don't have all the answers, and by the time they do bring up an important issue, their company may be in dire straits, and it is too late. Then they tell us that they are quitting the group because they are too busy running their company.

Often the real reason for quitting is that they don't have the cash-flow to pay the membership fees or they say they "can't justify spending the money on the fees because they don't get anything from the group." But they *would* get something from the group if they would show up, open up, and be vulnerable.

WHERE TO FIND MENTORS

When you seek out a mentor, look for someone who is currently where you want to be in the future. Do not limit yourself by searching for someone in the same industry. You may be better off if they are not your competition, unless they are outside your market area. When I was trying to open and manage multiple locations, I looked for someone who owned a business in multiple locations and ended up speaking with someone in the restaurant industry. When I was trying to increase our level of customer service, I looked for someone whom I admired and whose company was renowned for excellent customer service. They were in the computer software industry.

Mentorships can be temporary and only last through an issue or project that you are trying to figure out. Sometimes a mentorship will last years, and your mentor will become like family. Having a great mentor can be a life-changing experience.

At one conference I attended, there was a short mentorship program that paired high school girls with seasoned businesswomen. One student asked, "What is something you wish you knew at my age?" One of the business owners replied, "That there are so many people out there willing to help if you ask." I have found this to be true in the business community. For the most part, when a business owner has achieved a certain level of success, they are excited and willing to help other business owners, if asked. I have been lucky to have found knowledgeable, kind people who have helped me along the way.

There also are ways to have *one-way mentorships* in which you simply stalk a company or CEO that you admire to get ideas for your company. With the advent of the Internet and social media, you can gain never-available-before access into what other top CEOs are thinking and doing. Many famous CEOs have LinkedIn, Twitter, and Facebook, on which they produce content consistently. Herb Kelleher of Southwest Airlines and Howard Schultz of Starbucks were my one-way mentorships. I was heavily influenced by reading everything I could get my hands on about these two leaders. Currently, I follow several thought leaders and companies whose brands I admire. Why reinvent the wheel if there is another company out there already doing something similar to what you want to do? Following thought leaders that are doing what you want to do is a great way to get ideas without needing to foster a real-life relationship.

END OF CHAPTER CHECKLIST

- ☐ Do I have someone I can trust, who has no ulterior motives, to give me solid business advice?
- ☐ Do I trust this person will tell me the truth, even if it isn't what I want to hear?
- ☐ Am I meeting with this person on a regular basis?
- ☐ Are there any local groups of business owners that I can join to receive honest feedback? (This does not include networking groups. Networking is great but is different from a mentorship group.)
- ☐ If I am in a business group or have a business mentor, am I comfortable with being vulnerable?
- ☐ If I am in a business group, do I turn off my phone, put away any electronic devices and truly be present to work on my business?

28

Two Tears in a Bucket

Growing up, I thought my dad was tough because he had such strong reactions. I confused boisterousness with strength. He was loud, and always pushing me to be strong. He knew that life could come at you hard, and he wanted to prepare me for it. I thought my mother, the quiet one, was weak. I correlated loud with strong and quiet with weak. But years later, I realized I was wrong.

After my dad sold me his company, my parents moved to the Gulf Coast and bought a home that, while not fancy, was nice, with three bedrooms, a large yard, and an ocean view. Restless in his retirement, my dad started driving around and buying up real estate along the coast. He had five rental properties by the time he was finished. Then Hurricane Ike, a monster storm, was preparing to hit the Gulf Coast. My parents had no experience with a hurricane of this magnitude.

Later, when newscasters reported on the approaching "killer storm" Ike, my parents were hesitant to leave. My dad didn't want to miss the excitement of watching the storm. Finally, they reluctantly packed their bags and came to stay with us in Houston, which is about ninety miles inland. Ike hit the coast during the night with lots of rain and heavy winds that resulted in the biggest power outage in American history, leaving close to three million homes without power. The next morning, when the clouds cleared and the sun came out, residents began to realize the magnitude of the damage.

My parents' home was on a peninsula and was cut off from the mainland due to flooding. When helicopters were finally able to do flyovers and send video footage back to the local news, we were devastated. It looked like nothing was left. The entire day we anxiously watched to see if we could figure out where my parents' home was on the video footage. My mother was quiet, absorbing everything. My dad grew angry.

On the third day of waiting for news, my dad woke up before dawn, packed a cooler, and left. My dad basically ran away from home—he had never taken off before. He was in his seventies and not in the best of health. I was freaking out, but my mom didn't seem rattled, as if he ran away from home every day. She said that he was going to drive up to Kentucky to see his sister, my aunt Linda, and then drive from there to Illinois to see his other sister, Aunt Suzie. He hadn't told her that plan, but "I just know your father."

Like clockwork, the next morning, Aunt Linda called to let us know that my dad had shown up. I could tell that Mom was worried about her house and the cats that had been left behind but was mostly worried about my dad. She was quiet and serious. On day four, we learned that residents could return as long as they had ID to prove they weren't looters. My mother, my soon-to-be husband, and I jumped in his truck and headed to the coast.

After proceeding through the police checkpoint and driving onto the Bolivar Peninsula, we could see that everything was gone. It was as though entire neighborhoods had never existed—all that was left were miles and miles of uninhabited, empty fields and shorelines.

We were driving down the road, looking at the open land with the ocean calmly lapping the shore, when we were interrupted by the GPS's robotic voice announcing, "You have arrived at your destination," yet all we could see was land and ocean. Even the foundation of my parents' home was gone. There were no neighbors' houses; there was nothing. We pulled off the street and got out of the car. My mom looked down, recognizing a paving stone. Her home, her pets, and everything she owned was gone. I watched as her small frame folded inwards as if she had been physically struck.

Then this petite woman threw her shoulders back, stood up straight, turned to us, and said, "I guess we'll need to call the insurance company." And with that, she made a decision to move forward.

At that moment, I thought of the first few lines of the Serenity Prayer used in Alcoholics Anonymous meetings. It had hung somewhere in our house when I was young, and I'd memorized it:

God, grant me the serenity to accept the things I cannot change,
The courage to change the things I can,
And the wisdom to know the difference.

My mother had the serenity to accept the things she could not change. My father had the courage to change the things he could. He was a fighter, and accepting things he could not change was not in his character. The storm was not something he could fight.

Years later, I spoke to my mom about that day and how impressed I was with her resilience. She shrugged as she washed dishes in the kitchen sink. "What choice did I have?"

She did have a choice. She could have fallen apart. She could have gone into a depression. She could have run away. But she didn't. She put one foot in front of the other and moved forward. No amount of tears could bring her house out of the sea. My mother, the quiet one who always seemed to be in my dad's larger-than-life shadow, is the strongest person I know.

STRENGTHEN YOUR STRESS MUSCLE

Stress: It is something business owners eat for breakfast each day.

My husband, John, developed a theory that everyone has a "stress muscle," and the more you use it, the stronger it becomes. As you move through life's situations, if you practice using your stress muscle, you can strengthen the muscle.

As a leader, you need to stay calm and measured: The team is looking at you to gauge the severity of situations. It is OK to show emotion—doing so helps your team connect with you—but you should do so in a strategic way. They should see when you are disappointed, sad, or even upset, but you should never lose control or freak out. You must stay calm in stressful situations if you want your team to remain calm. And the more stress you face, the better you'll get at remaining calm in stressful situations.

My six-year-old daughter came home from first grade one day in tears. She exclaimed that this had been the worst day of her *entire life*. After my prodding, she recounted how during lunch she was walking with her tray in the middle of the lunchroom and tripped. Her food went everywhere. She was mortified.

It is easy to dismiss her feelings because, as an adult, dropping some food on the floor isn't that big of a deal, but in her short six-year life span, this was a huge deal. She hadn't developed her stress muscle. Stress is relative. A seasoned business owner who has exercised their stress muscle by dealing with more stressful events during their career will be less stressed than a new business owner just starting out.

STRESS AS FUEL

Think of stress as *gasoline:* You can throw a match at it, and it will catch fire, or you can channel it and put it in your car to use as fuel to get you somewhere. When you arrive at the office, and it seems like you lost it all, you have a choice. You can let the stress paralyze you, or worse, demobilize you with negative emotions, or you can use stress as fuel and turn it into energy to mitigate the stressful issue. You can throw your shoulders back and move forward with a plan.

Many religions practice a way to "let go" if you experience something difficult. In Christianity, they say, "It is in God's hands." In Buddhism, you meditate and learn to free your mind. In one of my favorite books, *Midnight in the Garden of Good and Evil*, The Lady Chablis advises, "Two tears in a bucket, motherfuck it." My mother would say, "It is what it is. Life keeps marching on."

The sooner you make the decision to accept a challenge as either *unable to be changed* or as *a problem to solve* (and then start fixing it), the happier you will be.

THE FUCK IT OR FIX IT METHOD OF HANDLING STRESS

We can represent the Fuck It or Fix It Method of handling stress using a J Curve, which was employed in chapter ten. The horizontal axis represents time and the vertical axis represents mood. When something horrible happens, your first instinct may be to freak out. If you never experience that feeling, you wouldn't be normal. These initial overwhelming feelings are going to hit you in the gut like a punch.

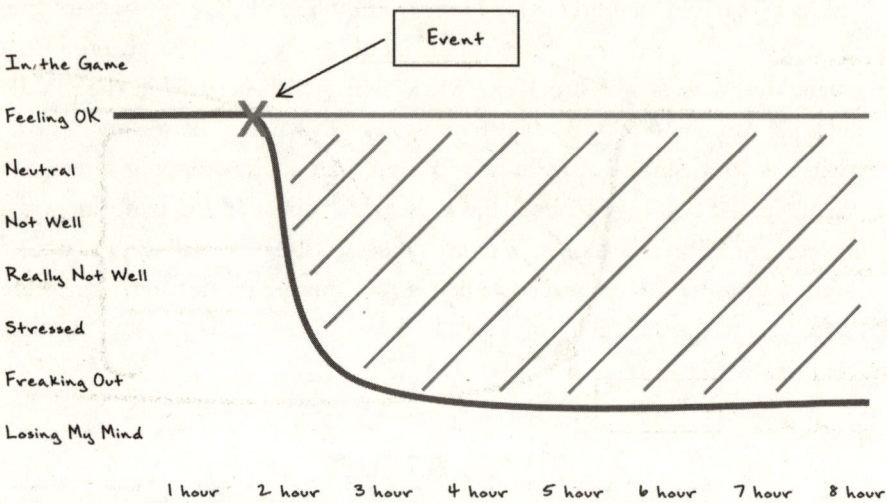

Separate the event that is happening from how you react. To do so, create space between the event and the reaction. A pause. Try to slow things down. Watch or listen to what is happening, wait to feel an emotion, and sit there for a while noticing what you are feeling, instead of reacting. You can do this by breathing deeply.

In my case, I engage in an inner dialogue that goes something like this:

Initial Freak Out: "OK. I can't believe this happened. This is horrible. OMG, what am I going to do?"

Then I breathe and ask myself, "Can I change what happened? Can I lessen the effect of what happened? Is there anything I can do?"

If the answer is *no*, I say, "Fuck it. It is what it is." You have to learn to accept that there is absolutely nothing you can do. Learning to accept things and move forward quickly is a skill you can develop. When you master this skill, you will have greater peace of mind.

If the answer is *yes, you can change something*, you should go in for a fight. When you start engaging in proactive actions to resolve a problem, it will lessen your stress. This is when you can channel the stress into fuel to create action.

The more I practice my Fuck It or Fix It Method, the more I can decrease the dip in the J Curve. The shorter the dip in the J Curve, the less I feel stressed and the more I am able to be the rock my team and family needs me to be.

TWO TEARS IN A BUCKET

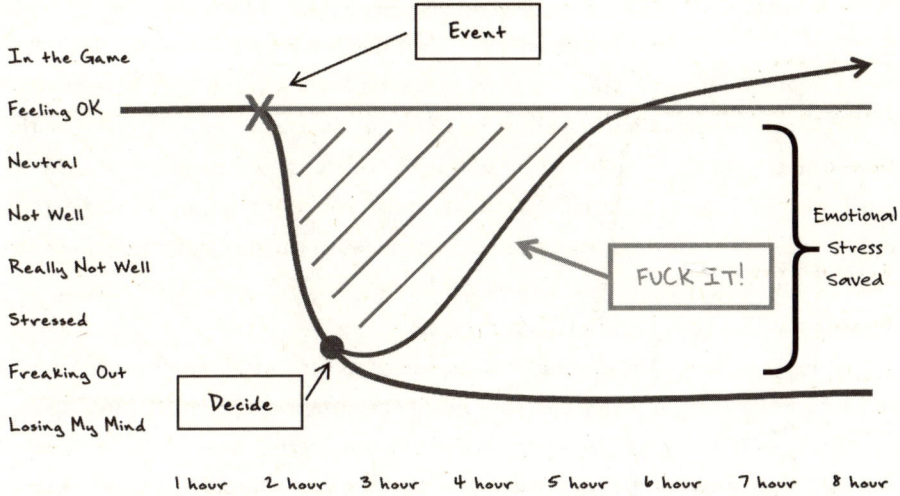

When I drive to work in the morning, I cross over a train track. Every once in a while, I will get stuck at the railroad crossing while an incredibly long train passes. This inevitably makes me late for my huddle meeting with the team. I hate being late, but allowing myself to get frustrated is a complete waste of energy. The train is just an event, even though I want to take it personally: *Why is this happening to me?* The fact is that it isn't happening to me—it is just happening. I can't make the train disappear. I can't levitate and go over it. There is nothing I can do to change the outcome of this particular event. Tomorrow, I can leave earlier, but today I need to decide to accept my circumstances and not allow this event to create negative energy that will ultimately get me nowhere.

Emotional fortitude is the ability to choose how you will feel in response to an event.

The ability to handle stress will give you the freedom to be content regardless of the chaos around you. The ability to stay calm under pressure is the ultimate mark of a strong, effective leader.

Here is an exercise to practice when you are driving home from a difficult day at work. As you process your day's events, ask yourself, *Can I change what happened today? Can I lessen the effect of what happened? Is there anything I can do?* Then ask yourself one more question: *Can it wait until tomorrow?*

Sometimes it can't, and as a small business owner, you might have to send some emails or make some calls when you get home. However, most of the time, the day-to-day issues can be left at the office, and a phone call can wait until the morning. It is better that way because you're tired, and if you sleep on it, you will have a fresh perspective and new ideas in the morning. Leaving your work problems at the door when you get home is a choice, and if you make that choice, you and your family will be happier.

When you are at the office and someone comes in to give you horrible news, remember my little seventy-year-old mom standing on the coast, looking out at the sea, and realizing that every possession she owned was gone. She didn't yell. She didn't cry. She didn't blame anyone. She stood up tall and got to work.

END OF CHAPTER CHECKLIST

- ☐ How do I currently process stress?
  - — Ignore it and bottle it up inside to the point that it can cause physical illness.
  - — Lash out and get angry at people around me.
  - — Experience the feeling and then decide if I should act on it or accept what happened as a part of life and move on.
- ☐ How do I show up to my team during stressful moments? Can they count on me to stay calm and levelheaded?
- ☐ Do I bring stress from work home to my family? Does work stress negatively affect my family life?
- ☐ Can I use stress as a fuel to solve fixable problems?
- ☐ Can I learn to let go of stress when I determine the problems that aren't fixable?

29
The Daily Grind

> Most folks are about as happy as they
> make their minds up to be.
> **—Abe Lincoln**

One day, after my dad had retired in his eighties, he was sitting in his easy chair when he heard the engine of a big truck pull up outside his beach house. He looked out his window and was delighted to see a 3 Men Mover's crew moving in his new neighbors. He dragged his chair over to the window and watched with excitement as the crew moved pieces of furniture up and down the exterior stairs. He never thought he would miss being out on a truck working, but he did. He looked back at the years he spent fighting and struggling with a feeling of nostalgia.

When your workday seems particularly crazy, you might be like my dad and dream about the day when you can put your business, and all the problems that come with it, behind you and move on to a more serene life. But also, like my dad, when years of struggle are far behind you, you may find that you actually miss those challenges. For him the grass was always greener on the other side. He longed for retirement. And when he finally got to kick back in his easy chair, he missed working.

Remember what we learned earlier about the word *regret* being the saddest word in the English language? It is my hope that the advice in this book will help you enjoy running your company. Yes, some days feel overwhelming, but if you have the right strategies to handle tough situations, business ownership can be one of the greatest rewards in life.

Enjoy the grind!

EPILOGUE

John David Fischer

Few men become legends in their lifetimes. My dad, John David Fischer, was just that for all who knew him. He was referred to by different nicknames over the years: the Maytown Rooster, Wolfman Jack, and simply Jacky to his family. But he will be remembered by most as the Kingfish because he grew up along the Rock River, and he was a king among men. He was known for many things, but he was unforgettable for his ability to fight and never give up, and his ability to love unconditionally.

He was born on September 25, 1935, in Sublette, Illinois, during the Great Depression. He was the son of John Howard Fischer and Pauline Reniff Fischer. He was the oldest of five siblings. The Kingfish learned to fight from his father, who had a temper and a fondness for drinking. He learned to love from his mother, who was a nurse and who, through her resilience and hard work, held the family together.

He had a rough life. He watched his mother struggle to support five kids during the Depression while his father stayed out all night drinking up his paychecks. His dad was abusive, and for some reason—perhaps because he was the oldest—my dad ended up bearing the brunt of his father's abuse.

His first job was setting bowling pins at a bowling alley when he was in the fourth grade. He attended St. Anne's Catholic School, where he was constantly in trouble and punished by the nuns who thought they could make him respect authority by striking his hands with rulers and making him hold Bibles with outstretched arms for long periods of time, but that made things worse.

Later, he went to Amboy High School, but left school and earned his GED. Liking the water, he decided to join the Navy, but not wanting to be told what to do, the Kingfish would jump overboard and got in trouble for fighting. He once jumped off the side of a destroyer in the port of Hong Kong to go out on the town. The current was so strong it almost swept him away. Luckily, he was fished out and survived.

He told me several stories about his time in the Navy. One was about his friend Fast Hands Freddie Nelson, who was Black, an amateur Navy boxer. When a bartender refused to serve Freddie, my dad challenged him to a fight. Freddie didn't want any trouble and just wanted to find another bar. After going AWOL a few times on benders, my dad finally was thrown out of the military.

After the Navy, he roamed across the US and worked over one hundred blue-collar jobs. He was restless and lost. He worked in the fields, on assembly lines, and in construction. He didn't need to make much money—just enough to go honky-tonking. He was a handsome man, six feet tall, with clear blue eyes and long, wavy hair. He was a pool shark, an amazing dancer, and a fighter.

The stories about his life seemed like scenes from a Quentin Tarantino movie, like how he once stole a Miller Lite truck and when the police pulled him off a water tower. A bartender pulled a gun on him and asked him to leave a bar in New Orleans. He would stay out all night and howl at the moon but was never late for work.

He was in a bar in New Orleans when JFK was shot. The news came across the TV, and everyone began cheering while he sat brokenhearted.

In his thirties, he moved back to the town he grew up in, Dixon, Illinois. During this time, his best friend, Starkey, was shot by a wealthy man in town, in front of many witnesses, who got off on all charges without serving a day in jail.

While in Dixon, he met my mom in a bar and fell madly in love. When my mom saw him from across the room, she thought he looked like Marlon Brando. Her friends later asked, "What the hell do you see in that wild man?" And she would reply, "He is not afraid to feel things. When he's happy, he laughs, and when he's sad, he cries." Shirley was in love too.

They married on December 30, 1972, in Dixon. Now the Kingfish really had something to fight for.

He started several companies, mostly in sales, mostly on shoestring budgets, all of them failing but one.

He was so acutely aware of his situation in life and the real possibility that he and my mother might end up destitute in their old age that he was always on edge. He was sensitive and carried around the pain of all the inhumane things he had seen throughout his lifetime. He always had a soft spot for the underdog—his single mother, his Black friend.

Moving to Houston was an opportunity for him to become anonymous, escape his reputation, and start over. He could make a clean break.

He worked harder than any person I have ever met. There was an angst in him when he worked. His movements were not only rushed but aggressive and desperate. You could almost hear a roar coming from within him. He was like a dog on a bone when he was trying to get something done. Tenacious. By the time I came on the scene, he was working as though time were running out.

He was an intelligent man, but he could never find a job that recognized him for this talent. Work gives life purpose, but his work always left him feeling broken.

Every time he found himself broke, he would come back fighting harder. His moving company, 3 Men Movers, would grow into a multimillion-dollar corporation. Even though he became wealthy and successful, he never forgot his struggles and was always willing to help others. He was everyone's cornerman. He would lecture, motivate, and push people back into the ring of life to fight another round. He loaned out and gave away millions of dollars to help his family, friends, and employees. Sometimes it was to make ends meet; other times he would finance the down payment for a new home or help someone start their own business.

With my parents having been poor all their lives, my mom would worry that his big heart would cost him, because at times people would take advantage of him. The Kingfish would say, "I would rather be known for people taking advantage of me than ever known for taking advantage of anyone." That is the way he lived his life.

In 2003, his stroke and other health issues pushed him into early retirement. He struggled for his entire life, hoping that someday it would pay off so he would be able to relax. When he finally made it to retirement, he was miserable. He didn't know how to relax. He was restless, grouchy, and depressed and felt that his life lacked purpose and direction. He didn't know what to do with himself. He missed the fight. He sat in his chair, stared out at the ocean, and stewed.

In 2015, when he was eighty, he and my mother bought a home along the Rock River and moved back to their childhood town of Dixon. He had spent the first forty years of his life in the North and the second forty years in Texas, and now he was moving back to his original home. When he returned, people still remembered him after all those years. He was still a legend around those parts, and now he had returned, finally a success.

He loved the attention when people would recognize him on the street and come up to talk to him. He loved going down to the Alley Loop, a tavern that ran out of a building he bought downtown, for a beer while seeing old friends. His eyes began to get their twinkle back. After eighty years, he finally was content in life.

On a visit with my parents, I walked into the Alley Loop, and everyone recognized me. My dad constantly had been showing photos of me, and they would politely glance at them and out of obligation say, "Oh, she is beautiful." My dad would shout back, "That isn't important! It is her heart. She has a beautiful heart."

The last time I saw him, he spoke slowly and looked me straight in the eyes to be sure I knew he was serious: "You know I love you? I'm proud of you." It was worth the forty-year wait.

Toward the end of his life, he developed Parkinson's disease, which made it hard for him to walk, and on August 21, 2016, he fell. He was rushed to the hospital. The ICU doctors tried to save him by hooking him up to machines, tying his arms down to keep him from pulling out the IVs and breathing equipment.

But my dad was a fighter; nobody ties down the Kingfish. He fought for days against the restraints until the doctors finally said there was no hope, unhooking him from the machines and untying him. By then, tired from fighting his whole life, he settled into a deep sleep. They transferred him to his home and put him in bed facing the Rock River. In the early hours of August 28, my brother, Patrick, whispered in his ear, "You are the Kingfish, the king of all the river fish," and then my dad smiled. Later that day, surrounded by love, he slipped away.

ACKNOWLEDGMENTS

A special thanks to: All my prereaders: Kate Noons; Mitch Gonzalez; Raymond Kerkvliet; my mom, Shirley Fischer; and my husband, John Ofield.

My mentors: Robin Stanaland, who is a genius of knowing just the right questions to ask. William Peery, who taught me sage old-school Business 101. Raymond Huddlton, who told me that participating in a recession is optional. The late Margret Cording, who said the most important word a businessperson can say is "no."

Erik Dane, who taught me about what employees need.

Tom Bourne for helping me find inner strength.

Speakers Eric Coryell, Nick Satchell, and the late Kraig Kramers.

Vistage 812—thanks for calling me on my shit.

Gino Wickman for writing the book *Traction*.

My first editor, Jeff Karon, for smoothing out the rough edges and creating illustrations to make the material easier to understand.

Rice University for taking a chance on a college dropout.

The drivers at 3 Men Movers for signing your names on the petition that changed my life. You make me proud.

The employees at 3 Men Movers who've taught me so much. I can't name y'all, but those of you who have been with me over ten years—Arny Sanchez, Claudia Ramirez, Norma De La Vina—it isn't easy embracing change, but y'all do it with grace. And my Leadership Team, thanks for holding down the fort while I wrote this book. Gor Avagyan, Jasmine Lewis, Kathryn Cheung, Mitch Gonzalez, Tomas Prestamo, Natasha Martinez, and Carla Saud.

My customers, your home is sacred. Thank you for trusting us.

All the folks at BenBella Books for your confidence and patience. A very special thanks to Matt Holt for believing I had something worth saying. Thank you to my agent, Kevin Anderson.

My siblings, Michael McConnell, Kelly Brady, Chris McConnell, and Patrick McConnell, for toughening me up.

My kids, Alex and Kate Noons, for always being supportive and understanding of my work. It is an honor to be your mom.

My husband, who heard way too many times, "I have to work on my book today." I am a better human because of you, and I am grateful to have you by my side.

ABOUT THE AUTHOR

Photo by Molly Dougherty

Jacky Fischer grew up working in a multitude of crazy family businesses and is quite sure her parents broke every child labor law.

As an art school dropout, she took over 3 Men Movers in 2003, growing the company from a mom-and-pop business to a multimillion-dollar company with locations throughout Texas. 3 Men Movers has consistently grown at a rate of over four times the industry average. She went back to school and received her MBA from Rice University in 2011.

Her passion is to help small business owners grow by using business methods based on creating kind and accountable work environments. She can be reached on LinkedIn or at jackyfischer.com.